THE SALESFORCE CONSULTANT'S GUIDE

TOOLS TO IMPLEMENT OR IMPROVE YOUR CLIENT'S SALESFORCE SOLUTION

Heather Negley

Apress®

The Salesforce Consultant's Guide: Tools to Implement or Improve Your Client's Salesforce Solution

Heather Negley
Fairfax, VA, USA

ISBN-13 (pbk): 978-1-4842-7959-5 ISBN-13 (electronic): 978-1-4842-7960-1
https://doi.org/10.1007/978-1-4842-7960-1

Managing Director, Apress Media LLC: Welmoed Spahr
Acquisitions Editor: Susan McDermott
Development Editor: Laura Berendson
Coordinating Editor: Jessica Vakili

Distributed to the book trade worldwide by Springer Science+Business Media New York, 233 Spring Street, 6th Floor, New York, NY 10013. Phone 1-800-SPRINGER, fax (201) 348-4505, e-mail orders-ny@springer-sbm.com, or visit www.springeronline.com. Apress Media, LLC is a California LLC and the sole member (owner) is Springer Science + Business Media Finance Inc (SSBM Finance Inc). SSBM Finance Inc is a **Delaware** corporation.

For information on translations, please e-mail booktranslations@springernature.com; for reprint, paperback, or audio rights, please e-mail bookpermissions@springernature.com.

Apress titles may be purchased in bulk for academic, corporate, or promotional use. eBook versions and licenses are also available for most titles. For more information, reference our Print and eBook Bulk Sales web page at www.apress.com/bulk-sales.

Any source code or other supplementary material referenced by the author in this book is available to readers on the GitHub repository: https://github.com/Apress/Salesforce-Consultant's-Guide. For more detailed information, please visit www.apress.com/source-code.

Printed on acid-free paper

To my mother, Joy Durkin, and my Aunt Mary (Cookie) Durkin for always loving and supporting me.

Contents

About the Author

Heather Negley is an independent Salesforce consultant currently working with Simplus. She also mentors and teaches Salesforce professionals on consulting best practices. She is a results-driven, senior leader with more than 25 years of software, automation, and web experience in the private sector, non-profits, and government. She is Salesforce and PMP certified and has worked on dozens of Salesforce implementations as a technology lead, project manager, business analyst, change manager, and solution and business architect. Heather lives in Virginia with her husband James and their two daughters, Ella and Gwyneth.

About the Technical Reviewer

David Masri founded Gluon Digital in 2020 with the goal of promoting data migration and integration best practices to the Salesforce Ohana. Prior to founding Gluon Digital, Dave spent years working with data and with Salesforce. He has been involved in dozens of Salesforce data migration and integration projects and has used that experience to run numerous training programs for aspiring integration/migration specialists and then ultimately authored a book (*Developing Data Migrations and Integrations with Salesforce*) on the subject.

Previously Dave was the director of professional services at Plative, a Salesforce Silver Partner. Before that he was the technical director of data strategy and architecture for Capgemini Invent's Salesforce Practice. He has more than 20 years of hands-on experience building integrated ERP, BI, e-commerce, and CRM systems, and for the past seven years has worked exclusively with the Salesforce platform. Dave holds more than ten professional certifications, including nine Salesforce certifications, the Project Management Professional (PMP), and Google's Data Engineer Certification. David is a lifelong New Yorker, born and raised in Brooklyn, where he currently lives with his loving wife Nancy and their kids, Joey, Adam, Ally, and Lilly.

Acknowledgments

First and foremost I would like to thank my family for their support and encouragement during the months I spent writing this book. Each of you live in my heart.

I would also like to thank Wendy, Kai and Behzad for generously sharing your stories with me and the readers. Your stories create a texture that I could not have produced alone. A special thank you to David Masri, my technical editor, whose advice and detailed eye made this book better. And also thanks to my cousin, Tres, for his mentorship and advice.

Thank you to the team at Apress. You have made this a fantastic journey. Thank you, Susan for taking a chance on me and for Jessica for ensuring a smooth writing process and making it an enjoyable experience from start to finish.

And thank you to my friends for your encouragement and inspiration.

Introduction

In 2013, I was a new mother with two small children. I had only been out of the workforce for four years, but during that time a lot had changed in the world, and I wasn't sure what I wanted to do next. My journey into the Salesforce ecosystem was a little serendipitous. I met a recruiter at a networking event on Big Data in downtown Washington, DC, and was hired at a consulting company that was having a Salesforce bootcamp. Now eight years later, I have been on more than 30 Salesforce delivery projects in technical and nontechnical roles.

The intention of this book is to give new consultants a guide that you can refer to as you enter the Salesforce ecosystem and start project work. The book is divided into four parts.

- Part 1: Where to Start
- Part 2: Preparing for a Software Project
- Part 3: Stages of a Project
- Part 4: Consulting Skills

Chapter 1 is intended to orient you to the Salesforce ecosystem by giving you an overview of Salesforce, the company, and how it got its start, including an explanation of the Salesforce ecosystem and the platforms that are part of it.

Chapter 2 includes an overview of the best learning and community resources as well as mentoring programs, conferences, and regional events.

Chapter 3 has tips on how to get job experience through volunteering if you are certified but have not actually worked on a project. This is a common dilemma when all the job postings require experience. This chapter will help guide you to places that need Salesforce help.

Chapter 4 is a primer on the evolution of software development. It is intended to give you context and historical information on the incarnations of creating software. Salesforce projects usually support digital modernization strategies and with these strategies come automation. This chapter explains why humans can and should still work with automated systems. Software development lifecycles are frameworks to plan, implement, test, deploy, and maintain software, and details around the popular frameworks of Waterfall and Agile are also discussed.

Chapter 5 covers all the project roles that you have to choose from while working on a Salesforce project. From project managers to solution architects and developers, each role is defined in detail. An explanation of the job function of a consultant as a whole is also explained and how any role can be a consultant.

Chapter 6 explains the presales process and how you actually get staffed on a project. You will learn what being on the bench means as well as the difference between a centralized and decentralized staffing model. Also, there are tips for attending a sales hand-off meeting and what type of information to look for and what questions to ask.

Chapter 7 kicks off the stages of a project with Ramp-Up, which means how to get prepared for a project. It spans topics such as travel tips to understanding utilization expectations to knowing your role.

In Chapter 8, we finally start a project with a synopsis of Kickoff and Discovery. You will learn interpersonal do's and don'ts to remember during kickoff as well as understanding the client vision and use cases. A deep dive into Discovery covers business analysis, current and future state, process flows, and how to write user stories. Finally, the chapter wraps up with an overview of the stages of group development that include forming, storming, norming, performing, and adjourning. There are predictable times in a project when these stages are likely to occur and things you can do to identify and manage them.

In Chapter 9 we start building the application using the Agile process. You will learn about backlog refinement, sprint planning, and other Agile ceremonies. There is also a section on how to properly use visuals to communicate complex information in an easily digestible format. This chapter concludes with an overview of user acceptance testing and deployment.

The last part on consulting skills starts in Chapter 10 with the first soft skill of client management. Seven project archetypes or project patterns are discussed with tips on what to watch out for and strategies to help navigate these projects.

- The Hydra
- The Echo Chamber
- Swiss Cheese
- The Explorer
- The Rube Goldberg
- High Horse
- Stick in the Mud

Chapter 11 is all about communication and how to choose the right medium depending on the type of message that you want to deliver. There are also tips on how to listen well and tips for choosing the right word when speaking or writing. There is also an overview of Slack and how it has changed the way we communicate with each other at work.

Chapter 12 is an overview of emotional intelligence and how to understand how our emotions affect our project work. A review of Plutchik's Wheel of Emotions reveals that our emotions are interconnected. Emotional situations that occur on projects are discussed in the context of common scenarios such as encountering difficulties when a new group forms, making mistakes, becoming burned out, and getting removed from a project or fired from a firm. Perspectives on which emotional consulting tools to utilize are intended to help navigate these tough situations.

Critical thinking is covered in Chapter 13 with an overview of the steps to systematically solve problems through logic. Tips on learning how to gather information in an organized manner so you can analyze and evaluate it are discussed. Avoiding bias and being aware of how to manage information over-load are key concepts in this chapter. Finally, the chapter concludes with a look at some of the cognitive biases that you may encounter on a Salesforce project. This includes a link to an infographic with more than 180 cognitive biases that are out there.

Where to Start

Introduction to the Salesforce Ecosystem

This book was written for people who are Salesforce consultants and for people who would like to become Salesforce consultants—whether you are just starting your career, you are a stay-at-home parent thinking of going back to work, or you have already had one career and would like to try something new. I found Salesforce in the middle of my career and would like to share with you the knowledge that I have gathered from being a Salesforce consultant for nearly a decade on dozens of projects.

© Heather Negley 2022
H. Negley, *The Salesforce Consultant's Guide*,
https://doi.org/10.1007/978-1-4842-7960-1_1

In this book, I hope to provide you with the knowledge, resources, and tools that you will need to be successful. This book is divided into three sections. The first part introduces you to the Salesforce community that is referred to as an *ecosystem* and where you can go to find resources to help you get certified as well as places to go to gain experience.

The second part of the book gives you a perspective on the types of projects that you may be working on from a macro perspective. The history of automation and software development is intended to orient you and give you a basis of knowledge on how these types of projects came to be. You will also learn common project roles and typical sales and staffing processes in consulting firms as well as important information to receive from account executives to set you up for a successful project. The third part of the book covers the parts of a project and tips to maximize your effectiveness during each phase. The final part is an overview of soft skills for consultants, including communication, emotional intelligence, client management, critical thinking, and how to avoid burnout.

The Salesforce Ecosystem

The Salesforce community is referred to as an *ecosystem* because it best describes the vast array of consulting and integration partners, third-party app companies, and teachers who encircle Salesforce the company. Without this internetwork of synergistic pieces, Salesforce would not have as big a reach in the cloud computing software market. With more than 49,000 employees in 2020, Salesforce has a market cap of $193.55 billion as of March 10, 2021, and had revenue surpassing $17 billion for the fiscal year ending January 31, 2020.[1]

In fact, in a Salesforce-sponsored study, the International Data Corporation (IDC) predicted that by 2024, Salesforce and its ecosystem are expected to enable the creation of 4.2 million jobs worldwide. While keeping in mind that industry-sponsored studies tend to be biased toward their own product, this is still a huge prediction with a big impact on new job generation for a large number of people across a vast geographic area. So, given Salesforce's trajectory, the general sentiment is very clear: Salesforce jobs will be on the rise for several years to come.

Salesforce has been around for quite a while. It was started in 1999 in San Francisco by Marc Benioff who had been working at Oracle as a vice president. Marc partnered with Parker Harris, Dave Moellenhoff, and Frank Dominguez, and they created a software-as-a-service platform for customer relationship management and named it Salesforce. The company went public in 2004.[2]

One of the more interesting elements that has probably contributed to the company's success is the philanthropy model that Benioff coined the 1-1-1 model. It is designed to give back 1 percent of the company's equity, product, and employees' time to the ecosystem. As Benioff explains in his 2019 biography,[3] as his idea for starting the company was starting to take shape, he took a trip to India where he developed a spiritual intent to give back that was nurtured and influenced by Mata Amiritaanandamayi, a spiritual leader and humanitarian known as "the hugging saint." She ends all her programs by hugging all who attend and has hugged more than 40 million people worldwide.[4] When he met her on this trip and explained his business idea, she told him, "In your quest to succeed and make money, don't forget to do something for others." The 1-1-1 model is Benioff's practical application of this advice. I think that if Benioff had not been able to clearly translate this type of idealist intention into a succinct measurable goal, then Salesforce would not be the type of company it is today.

Benioff's knack for taking abstract concepts and defining them and scaling them around the Salesforce brand is evidenced again with the cultural concept he created for Salesforce called Ohana, which means "family" in Hawaiian. The Salesforce ecosystem is often referred to as the Ohana. He intentionally

[1] "Salesforce, Inc Financial Statements 2005-2021 | CRM." www.macrotrends.net. Retrieved March 11, 2021.
[2] https://www.salesforce.com/news/stories/the-history-of-salesforce/#:~:text=2004,million%20at%20%2411%20per%20share.
[3] Trailblazer, Marc Benioff
[4] http://www.embracingtheworld.org/about-amma/

chose this concept rather than a team type of idea that many other companies adopt to describe culture because Ohana encapsulates ethos or the values of family instead of a more stripped-down idea of a generic team.[5] There is a reason that so many people in the world now use Salesforce and want to learn it, and I believe that these two aspects, the 1-1-1 model and Ohana, are a large part of it. As you start your Salesforce journey, you will quickly find other people in the ecosystem who want to help you to succeed, and finding help will come easily. The Ohana concept has set the mood for the ecosystem, and Benioff is consistently refining it as Salesforce grows, extending it to partners and customers.

The Salesforce ecosystem is more than four times larger than Salesforce itself,[6] and by 2024, it will be nearly six times bigger. It is broken into three distinct organization types. But maybe I should start with why it is referred to as an *ecosystem* in the first place. As a Salesforce consultant, I have attended many meetings where Salesforce professionals really do introduce themselves to each other by indicating how long they have worked in the ecosystem. The introduction usually sounds something along the lines of "Hi, my name is Jackie, and I have been in the ecosystem for seven years." It is often just referred to as "the ecosystem," and the longer you have worked in it, the better. It doesn't matter how many jobs you have had, only that you have worked in the ecosystem. The more time, the more inferred clout and experience that you have. Being part of the Salesforce "ecosystem" means you have worked in an industry that makes its revenue by either consulting, building third-party apps, or teaching Salesforce, and not necessarily as an employee of Salesforce.

But back to the types of organizations. First, there are pure Salesforce customers or end users. These are industry companies that implement and manage their Salesforce organization in-house. The typical roles in this type of organization are administrator, developer, and business analyst. I will explain roles in more detail in Chapter 5. But the important thing to know at this point is that people who work for an end-user organization play a part in planning the roadmap for building out their Salesforce instance and are not consultants, so if you want to work as a consultant, this is not the type of organization that you would want to look for. The main focus of this guidebook is on consulting jobs.

The next type of organization is the Salesforce partner, sometimes referred to as an *implementation partner* or *consulting partner* or even as *system integrators* (SIs), because they help customers implement their business rules and

---

[5] Trailblazer, page 130–132.
[6] https://www.salesforce.com/content/dam/web/en_us/www/documents/reports/idc-salesforce-economy-report.pdf

processes and migrate their data into the platform. Some of the most popular roles in this type of organization are technofunctional consultants, developers, and functional consultants.

The last type is the independent software vendors (ISVs). These are organizations that build software on the platform, and typical roles include developer, technical and functional consultant, and administrator.

The Platform

As I said earlier, Salesforce is a software-as-a-service platform for customer relationship management. Software-as-a-service means that the software is delivered over the Internet, and the service provider, in this case Salesforce, hosts the applications. You might also see it written as SaaS. Salesforce is both the name of the company and the name of the flagship product. Salesforce is made up of subproducts called *clouds* such as Sales Cloud, Service Cloud, et al. There are many other separate products as well such as Mulesoft, Tableau, and Slack, to name just a few.

Salesforce stores customer data using a multitenant architecture, which means that you share server space with other customers. Think of it as an apartment building that has separate apartments. Everyone shares the same building but has their own space in the building. Multitenant is similar and is popular because it saves companies costs on buying and managing their own servers.

Since Salesforce is a platform, this means users can build many applications inside their spaces or organizations. You may also hear them referred to as *orgs*. As mentioned, Salesforce is primarily known as a customer relationship management database. This means that the platform comes with standard objects named for a user managing their sales leads and opportunities. Sales Cloud is the name of the product on the platform with the collection of objects that serves this purpose. Standard objects are contacts, accounts, leads, and opportunities. It also gives users the ability to create their own custom objects. The tabular interface for interacting with the database objects and related lists and views is visually appealing.

Salesforce creates relationships between objects and brands the apps as *clouds* for specific industries or business processes. Some product examples include Sales Cloud, Service Cloud, Marketing Cloud, Pardot, and Experience Cloud, to name a few. Customers buy the license for the product that fits their business needs.

In the next chapter, you will learn about ways to find a job as a Salesforce consultant both with and without Salesforce experience. You will learn about the Salesforce mentoring program and how to volunteer to gain the experience needed to land a job.

Summary

Salesforce began in 1999 and has grown into a vast ecosystem with an increasing number of job opportunities. It has a robust philanthropic strategic vision called the 1-1-1 model and a culture based on family values called Ohana.

The Salesforce ecosystem consists of three types of organizations: Salesforce customers, Salesforce partners, and independent software vendors.

Salesforce is a software-as-a-service platform that sells many apps that come with standard objects depending on the license type. The relationships between the objects create a data model that serve as a starting point for the application. Changes to the data model can be made by creating custom objects.

Resources

History of Salesforce, `https://www.salesforce.com/news/stories/the-history-of-salesforce/#:~:text=The%20company%20now%20has%201.5,150%2C000%20customers%20and%2016%2C000%20employees`

Benioff, Marc, and Langley, Monica, Trailblazer: the Power of Business as the Greatest Platform for Change

Salesforce Learning

In this chapter, you will discover the best learning resources and community resources to aid your learning. Finding a mentor is an important first step, and the Trailblazer Mentorship program makes it easy to find one.

There are many free learning resources in the ecosystem to help you prepare for your first certification. The Salesforce Administrator certification is the most common first certification to acquire.

There are also many paid learning resources for all different budgets. Finding a learning community to engage in is critical to support your learning. It is both important for knowledge growth and important because it helps you make connections with people in the ecosystem, which is important once you find a job, as you will see in Chapter 3.

Tapping into key learning resources can help you achieve your goals in the Salesforce ecosystem. Learning Salesforce is an important piece in the journey of becoming a knowledgeable Salesforce consultant. As you will read in Chapter 5, each role has its own learning path. A Salesforce consultant obtains knowledge germane to their roles from project work and also from technology training. Consultants work on projects that are often short-term. This allows a lot of experiences to accumulate in a short period of time. Consultants then use this knowledge to help clients on future projects.

© Heather Negley 2022
H. Negley, *The Salesforce Consultant's Guide*,
https://doi.org/10.1007/978-1-4842-7960-1_2

If you are just starting out, being able to identify the things you don't know and figuring out the best processes for learning them is key to both getting experience and landing a job. This chapter has several resources to help you find the right learning sources.

Being a good Salesforce consultant consists of three overlapping parts: learning, community, and a job (see Figure 2-1). In this section, I will explain learning and community and their overlap with learning communities. Chapter 3 will focus on strategies and resources for finding a job and the overlap with job communities. Chapter 5 has more resources based on your specific project role.

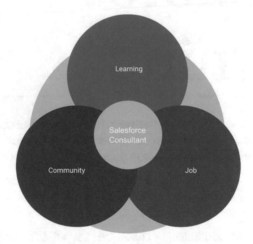

Figure 2-1. Three parts of being a Salesforce consultant

Historically speaking, we are living in a time of enormous prosperity with many opportunities. One of the reasons there is so much demand is because Salesforce has had huge success spreading the platform across the world, and that is opening up opportunities for many people. You can get a job working from home using your intellect to contribute to a team that is trying to solve problems and innovate. That is pretty exciting.

The technology field is not a hard field to break into if you are willing to learn new things. It is an enormous industry that is constantly changing and innovating. There is always a need for people to learn the new technologies that are developed. If you are someone who has the desire and aptitude to learn and are curious about how things work, then your inexperience on the platform will not get in the way. The Salesforce platform teaches "clicks not code," which means that you learn how to configure an interface by navigating to the right section in an administration setup. This type of work is still considered development, and in fact Salesforce used to call people who did this type of work *developers*, but it fell out of use because it became confusing to distinguish this type of work from people who write code line by line. You do not have to learn how to write code to be a Salesforce consultant unless you want to, and if you do, then your role is considered to be a developer. You'll learn more about roles in Chapter 5.

Don't let your age hold you back either. There are plenty of jobs to go around for young and old. Older workers may have experience working with people, running meetings, and collaborating that will help as a consultant. If you are older than 55, you can also learn to be a Salesforce consultant and get a good job advising companies on how to solve their business problems. In fact, your life experience will come in handy. The technology might be new, but working with people is not, and solid industry experience is very much needed in the ecosystem. Whether it is on a team or communicating with a client, soft skills matter. I will describe soft skills in more detail in Part 4. Whether or not you have Salesforce experience should not keep you from exploring a career as a Salesforce consultant. There are ways to get experience that I will discuss in Chapter 3.

Mentoring

One of the first things you should do as you start to explore Salesforce is find a mentor. Mentors are good guides for anyone no matter the Salesforce experience level. Salesforces' Trailblazer Mentorship matches Salesforce ecosystem volunteers called *trailblazers* to those looking for guidance. Trailblazer is a generic term for anyone who spreads knowledge in the community. The program is worth joining because the people who volunteer to mentor are part of the Ohana community and want to help others. Remember, the Ohana community is a support system taken from the Hawaiian word for family. It extends beyond Salesforce the company to partners, which includes consultants as well as Salesforce customers and other people who use the platform.

I have participated in the program as a mentor and helped people with a variety of needs. Sometimes it helps to just talk through your goals out loud with another person to help solidify them. Mentors like to share their experiences and offer advice depending on your situation. Everyone has unique needs, and a mentor can hone in on yours quickly.

Some of the specific things that a mentor can help with is to look over your résumé. This may help you pull out your strengths and make sure that they are reflected in your résumé in a clear and concise way. Sometimes, we overlook our strengths, so I highly recommend talking with a mentor who asks you about you. Other things that a mentor may help with are giving you certification advice, job search advice, salary negotiation strategies, examining your online presence on LinkedIn, and making recommendations on personal branding.

Learning

A willingness to learn is important. Tech cycles are short, lasting just three to five years, so learning is important, and it is a constant.[1] You might spend a lot of time getting certified in a solution only to find five years later that the technology is different. This doesn't mean you shouldn't bother learning the technology that is popular now, but be flexible, curious, and adaptable, and remember that things are changing all the time. Being able to learn quickly and consistently is a skill and a huge benefit to doing this type of work. Every time a new project begins, see it as a new learning cycle starting.

There are many places to get Salesforce knowledge. There are free resources such as Trailhead, bootcamp programs, and learning competitions. As you choose your subject area of concentration, these resources continue in a more refined, deeper, and narrower scope with blogs, slack groups, podcasts, and webinars devoted to specific topics. There are role-specific resources in Chapter 5. If you are just starting out, this chapter has some good resources to get you started and oriented.

How much should you learn? The ecosystem is too large for one person to know everything, and that's okay. The goal is not to learn everything. The goal is to learn some and figure out what you are good at, what you like, what skills are in demand, and then align and move forward. Knowing where to go to find the answers is key.

---

[1] Zinn, Ray, Tech Cycle Survival, November 29, 2017, https://www.forbes.com/sites/forbestechcouncil/2017/11/29/tech-cycle-survival/?sh=6f811bf478ce

Free Learning

Here are some free learning opportunities.

Trailhead

Trailhead is the main salesforce learning portal and a good place to start. Bookmark it, because it is a valuable resource, and you will need to refer to it a lot. When I started my Salesforce journey, I didn't have Trailhead, but I wish that I had. It would have accelerated my learning. It is fun and helpful, but you can get lost in a maze of hours-long modules, and if you don't have a plan as to why you are in there, then it can turn into a time suck.

TRAILHEAD

Trailhead is gamified with points, badges, and superbadges. The badges have different levels called *trailblazer ranks*. They are Scout, Hiker, Explorer, Adventurer, Mountaineer, Expeditioner, and the highest Ranger.

Trailhead also has superbadges that will help you apply the knowledge with more in-depth, hands-on learning in the Trailhead playground, which is an area of sandboxes connected to the module that you can spin up easily and where you can practice configuring Salesforce orgs.

Even after you achieve Ranger, the learning never stops because you will use Trailhead to keep up with new features and technologies. There is even a Trailhead Live portal with a schedule of live events and on-demand videos on various featured content for newbies as well as detailed videos on the latest features in Trailhead. I talk more about events later in this chapter.

Free Bootcamp Programs

The Salesforce Pathfinder Program is a bootcamp program with Deloitte. It is a 16-week program. The program's goal is to teach technical and business skills to students. Proficiency in both of these areas is needed to excel as a Salesforce consultant. Part 3 explains some of the business skills that Salesforce consultants need.

Salesforce
PATHFINDER

The first eight weeks are focused on virtual Salesforce technical skills and Deloitte business training. After that, there are two weeks of in-person training and then time to study for the certification. Students do not have to pay to take the exams. The program is especially noteworthy because graduates gain access to job interviews. Apply at `https://pathfinder.salesforce.com`.

Pep Up Tech was founded in 2016 by Stephanie Herrera, Selina Suarez, and Rebe da la Paz as a solution to help underrepresented groups get trained in IT. The organization partners with colleges and holds a popular bootcamp program. You can apply for a course on their website. There are many volunteers from the Salesforce Ohana community who volunteer their time to support this nonprofit.

100 Days of Trailhead

In 2018, Jessica Murphy and Rachel Watson started a creative idea called 100 days of Trailhead.com. It is a community-supported program based on the concept of helping each other make and keep Salesforce learning goals using New Year's resolutions. To take part, you fill out a form on the website at the beginning of the year and sign up to spend the time learning by getting badges, superbadges, points, and certifications. There is also a fun leaderboard to keep track of your rank compared to other participants.

Paid Learning

There are more and more paid Salesforce classes offered by places other than Salesforce. Salesforce classes are by far the priciest at several thousand dollars a class. Trailhead Academy classes are given by Salesforce. If your place of employment is not offering to pay for the classes as part of their learning development program, then it may not be the most cost-effective way for you to learn. Many classes are offered by people who are influencers in the Salesforce ecosystem. Influencers are mostly people who have won Salesforce community awards, such a MVP or Golden Hoodie, and other leaders who have created Salesforce content such as blogs and podcasts.

Udemy is a paid online learning platform that has many types of classes. There are a lot of Salesforce classes on the platform. Mike Wheeler training courses are very popular.

Focus On Force offers paid but affordable training materials such as study guides and practice exams.

Supermums was started by Heather Black. The organization focuses on Salesforce training for moms and dads. The classes are pricier, but they also help with gaining experience and finding a job.

Francis Pindar's blog Radnip.com has useful informative information about the platform, and his site, Admintoarchitect.com, offers affordable training.

Certifications

The number of salesforce certifications keeps on growing. When I first started in 2013, there were around five. If I remember correctly, there was Salesforce Administrator, Advanced Admin Salesforce Developer, Salesforce Consultant, and Salesforce Service Cloud. Many people got all the certifications, and that was my goal for a while. But after a couple of years, Salesforce increased the number of certifications to 23, and I changed my mind, because it was unrealistic for me. However, I do know several people who got all 23.

Nowadays, there are more than 30 certifications, and getting all of them is not a goal I would recommend setting. It is becoming analogous to taking all the classes at college. It is better to start by taking general classes to introduce and orient you to the platform and then to specialize. An innovative society does not require you to become an expert in everything. You can have a high quality of life and a successful career by specializing. There is no need to try to be an expert at everything. And even if you try, you will probably become an expert in some things and a generalist in other areas.

If you are new to the ecosystem, the administrator exam is the first certification that most people get. You should start with this one if your goal is to be a Salesforce consultant. It is a prerequisite for a lot of other certifications including the consultant certifications such as Sales and Service Cloud among others. If you know you want to be a developer, then it is fine to start with Platform Developer 1. If you are unsure, then start with the Administrator certification; you can still get the developer certifications later.

Learning Communities

Remember, you are not alone when you set off to learn Salesforce. There are tons of resources and a friendly and helpful community of people who want you to succeed.

Trailblazer Community Groups

A Trailblazer is the name that Salesforce gives to people who complete badges in Trailhead. They are defined as people who love to learn and help others learn. MVPs are nominated from this group on a yearly basis. Trailblazers have their own community groups (https://trailblazercommunitygroups. com/). They are usually in-person meetups and are region based. This site functions as a portal to find a specific group you would like to join such as Salesforce Women in Tech that formed in 2010.

MVP Office Hours mvpofficehours.info

Salesforce MVPs created MVP Office Hours as an open forum for people to go to ask questions and get help on problems.

Salesforce Saturdays

The first Salesforce Saturday was started by one of the cofounders of Pep Up Tech. These are independent city-based meetups. To find one near you, the easiest thing to do is go to Meetup.com and search for a Salesforce Saturday near you. Attending one of these events is a good way to meet people in your local community who are learning Salesforce or work in the ecosystem.

Ohana Slack

Meighan Brodkey and Kevin Mikolajczak founded Ohana Slack, which is a Slack app (#OhanaSlack) for the Salesforce ecosystem. It is for everyone in the community including admins, devs, architects, specialists, and MVPs with all sorts of channels to explore.

Military

There are great training programs in the ecosystem for veterans and their spouses. The following are very popular.

Salesforce Military

Salesforce Military (https://veterans.force.com/s/) is a Salesforce program for active-duty, reserve, guard, veterans, and current military spouses in the United States, United Kingdom, Canada, Australia, and New Zealand. They give free training and help with job placement. Depending on how much time you have to spare, you can get certified in anywhere from one to six months.

There is also a Hiring Our Heroes and Salesforce Fellowship Program that provides 12 weeks of paid job training for certified Salesforce professionals (https://www.hiringourheroes.org/career-services/fellowships/industry-focus/salesforce/).

Mervis

Mervis (https://merivis.org/) is a nonprofit organization started by Hector Perez, Jr., to help veterans and military spouses through job training, mentorships, and job placement. Joining an admin cohort is a good place to start. The cohorts are $150, but there are ways to apply for scholarships.

Events

The following are some events.

Conferences

Dreamforce is the annual Salesforce conference held every year in San Francisco for clients and partners. It is one of the biggest tech conferences in the world. See https://www.salesforce.com/dreamforce/.

TrailheadDX is a Salesforce-sponsored conference for developers. See https://www.salesforce.com/trailheadx/.

Trailhead Events are webinars for admins and developers and other roles on a variety of Salesforce topics such as Salesforce fundamentals, essential habits for new admins, and how to build architecture diagrams. There are a wide variety of topics to choose from, and they have events posted months out. See `https://trailhead.salesforce.com/calendar?programs=trailhead`.

Regional Events

World Tours are smaller city events sponsored by Salesforce that take place all over the world. Clients and partners attend these events.

Community Conferences are put on by local groups. `https://trailhead.salesforce.com/community/conferences` is a directory of community conferences by region.

Summary

Salesforce consulting has three main parts: learning, community, and job. The first thing you should do if you want to be a Salesforce consultant is to join the mentorship program. Mentors can offer a lot of great guidance. A willingness to learn is important. Tech cycles are short, and learning is continuous. There are many free learning resources such as Trailhead, the Salesforce Pathfinder program, Pep Up Tech, and 100 Days of Trailhead. There are also a lot of paid learning resources such as Trailhead Academy, Udemy, Mike Wheeler training courses on Udemy, Focus On Force, Supermums, and Radnip.com.

It is not necessary to get all the Salesforce certifications but is important to get some. Salesforce Administrator is the one most people start off getting.

Engaging in learning communities is an important aspect of becoming a successful Salesforce consultant. There are many resources and a friendly and helpful community of people who want you to succeed. Look into Trailblazer community groups such as Women in Tech, MVP Office Hours, Salesforce Saturdays, and Ohana Slack. If you are a veteran, you can join Vetforce or Mervis.

There are also a plethora of virtual and in-person conferences such as Dreamforce, TrailheadDX, Trailhead Events, World Tours, and community conferences.

Resources

Trailblazer Mentorship Program, https://trailhead.salesforce.com/trailblazerconnect/mentorship

Trailhead, https://trailhead.salesforce.com

Trailhead Live Portal, https://trailhead.salesforce.com/live/

Salesforce Pathfinder, https://pathfinder.salesforce.com

Pep Up Tech, https://www.pepuptech.org/

Apply to Pep Up Tech, admissions@pepuptech.org

Salesforce Saturdays, https://www.meetup.com/topics/salesforce/

Trailhead Academy, https://trailhead.salesforce.com/en/academy

Udemy, https://www.udemy.com/

Focus on Force, https://focusonforce.com/

Supermums, https://supermums.org/

MVP Directory, https://trailhead.salesforce.com/mvp/#meet

100 Days of Trailhead, https://100daysoftrailhead.com

Francis Pindar's blog, https://www.radnip.com/

Francis Pindar's blog Radnip.com has useful informative information about the platform and his site, Admintoarchitect, https://admintoarchitect.com/

Salesforce Work Experience

There are many definitions of work experience. If your goal is to be a consultant, then Salesforce work experience means something specific. If you do not have this experience, then an easy way to get it is by volunteering. There are many organizations that facilitate matching volunteers with projects. Once you have project experience, working with a recruiter can speed up the job search.

Job Experience

So, you have taken your Administrator exam, and now you are certified. Great! Now, the job search begins. You start looking for a job, and everywhere you look you notice that every job posting requires experience. This age-old conundrum is never easy for any job seeker. It is the same question every time: "How am I supposed to get experience for this job when the job is what would give me experience? How do I start?"

From the employer's point of view, they want to hire someone who will bring value, and having experience is an assumed indicator of value. But what does lack of experience really mean? Well, it could mean that you have a job as a Salesforce administrator in an industry company, but you do not have project experience. Consultants do project work. They move from project to project.

© Heather Negley 2022
H. Negley, *The Salesforce Consultant's Guide*,
https://doi.org/10.1007/978-1-4842-7960-1_3

They do not work for one company for an extended period of time only undertaking operational work, which is often the case as a Salesforce administrator role. For example, I have been on more than 30 projects in the seven years that I have been a Salesforce consultant. Project experience gives you consulting experience because you move from one to another and take your experience with you to use when you advise the next client. Salesforce consultants may gain experience working for consulting firms or systems integrators. These types of companies are usually Salesforce partners that help companies configure, customize, or integrate the software based on specific business requirements.

Lack of experience can also mean that you could have experience in various roles on non-Salesforce projects such as a project manager or a business analyst but the job posting is looking for experience on Salesforce projects specifically. See Chapter 5 for a deep dive into roles. And while you may think that it shouldn't matter (after all, you have project experience), the fact is that more and more partners want project managers with experience managing Salesforce projects. Employers want project managers to have general knowledge of the parts of the Salesforce ecosystem and a basic understanding of the Salesforce platform. Most partners are probably fine with a basic knowledge of Sales Cloud or Service Cloud since these are core products. Getting the administrator certification should give you enough knowledge to have intelligent conversations with the solution architects and developers on your team.

A lack of experience could also mean that you do not have technical experience. You could be trying to make the switch from a business role to a more technical one. This can be harder to sell but not impossible. If you are someone like this, then you may have a capacity to understand technical systems from a general point of view. You have technical proficiency but are also really good at seeing the big picture. You may communicate very well with developers but lack the stamina to inspect and troubleshoot detailed scenarios over and over again until a single piece of functionality works. You can talk to developers who are detail based and communicate to them using analogies to show the bigger concepts and goals of the business users. In fact, sometimes developers build better code if someone can give them some context, but oftentimes they don't even ask because they are so detail oriented. This is a unique skill set that doesn't fit into traditional IT and business roles but is an important one. It means that you are a bridge and a good communicator. Working with a mentor to hone in on your personal experience and messaging around this concept is a worthwhile exercise.

Luckily, project experience is not that hard to obtain. As you will read in the next section, there are many ways to volunteer to get the experience you need.

Volunteer Work

Volunteering is a great way to gain experience. It is also known as pro bono work. If you don't have job experience, you can volunteer. If you have Salesforce certifications but no project experience or work experience, then volunteering is a great way to get experience. Nonprofits are always looking for this type of help because they have tight budgets.

Volunteer Resources

Let's take a look at some organizations that can help you find a volunteer opportunity.

Catch a Fire

Catch a Fire was founded in 2010 to facilitate matches between volunteers and nonprofits to strengthen the social good sector. The organization matches volunteers to opportunities based on skills. The service is not primarily for Salesforce, but it is possible to search for Salesforce project work on their website. Navigate to Find a Project under the Volunteer section and then follow the application prompts.

Browse for Salesforce opportunities at https://www.catchafire.org/.

Taproot Foundation

The Taproot Foundation is a nonprofit with the same type of pro bono mission as Catch a Fire. It began in 2001 and has helped more than 8,400 organizations. Like Catch a Fire, the opportunities are not all for Salesforce, but you can find Salesforce opportunities by going to the website https://www.taprootplus.org/opportunities and searching for *Salesforce* in the opportunity search.

VolunteerMatch

VolunteerMatch (`https://www.volunteermatch.org/search/index.jsp`) began in 1998 and has 117,000 active nonprofits. Volunteers can choose to volunteer based on location or virtually. Opportunities are not solely Salesforce based, but you can also browse by causes and search opportunities by typing in keywords like *Salesforce* to find the perfect match for you.

Points of Light Engage

Points of Light (`https://engage.pointsoflight.org/`) has an aggregator named Engage that collates volunteer opportunities and makes them available in a web search. Search for Salesforce opportunities and then click through to the posting on the source site and follow the specific directions. For example, the results of the search will show display postings on other sites such as Catch a Fire.

Idealist

Idealist (`https://www.idealist.org`) is a nonprofit that started in 1995, with the goal of helping people around the world live free and dignified lives. Their search engine aggregates volunteer opportunities from its own listings as well as sources from such as Volunteer Match, Points of Life, and AARP. Search for *Salesforce* in the search to see specific Salesforce volunteer opportunities.

Recruiters

Once you obtain Salesforce project experience, working with a recruiter can help you expedite the job search. Recruiters can help you learn how to present yourself and put your résumé together. There are many Salesforce recruiters. Some recruiters work for Salesforce partners, referred to as an *internal recruiter*, and recruit for the one company they work for. Other recruiters work for recruiting companies that specialize in Salesforce recruiting, and some work for recruiting companies that do not specialize at all but recruit for IT jobs in general. Since there are so many recruiters in the Salesforce space, it is important to do your due diligence and ask each specific recruiter who they work for and what they specialize in.

Recruiters can also help you with your résumé if you do not have a mentor. Often the ones who work at an independent company will offer these services versus the recruiters who work for the same company that they are recruiting for. Make sure that your goals are aligned with the roles that they are trying to fill if you ask for résumé feedback.

Recruiters can also help you find different working arrangements such as part-time or independent contracting at an hourly rate. They will help you find options if you are looking for a job with more flexibility than the traditional 9 to 5, 40-hour-a-week salary job. This type of employee is often referred to as a W2 employee named after the tax form for these types of employees.

Once you post your certifications and some job experience on your LinkedIn page, the recruiters will start sending you messages on LinkedIn. This is because you will come up in their searches when they start looking for resources to fill roles.

Of course, there are endless job aggregators who post Salesforce jobs, but I have found that the best jobs show up in LinkedIn through network connections. Oftentimes people in your network will post jobs that show up in your feed. This is another reason why making connections in the Salesforce ecosystem is so important.

Experience and certifications go a long way in the technology field, and Salesforce projects are no exception. In fact, it is possible to get by on these two strategies alone. I know several people without college degrees who are successful Salesforce consultants because they have certifications and continuous project experience.

Tapping into key learning resources can help you achieve your goals in the Salesforce ecosystem. For example, my friend, Wendy, used some of these resources to get back into the workforce after being away from it for 15 years. Despite having a BS in Electrical Engineering and more than 10 years of work experience, she was finding the job search challenging. Wendy decided to start studying for her Administrator certification and volunteered for her local community theater company which was using the free Salesforce Nonprofit Success Pack to keep track of their donations. After a few months, she found an internship as a Salesforce Administrator. She also signed up for RAD classes, the developer bootcamp given by Salesforce, and took Apex classes. Soon after, Wendy got a job as a Salesforce developer.

So, learning Salesforce is an important piece in the journey of becoming a knowledgeable Salesforce consultant. But being able to identify the things you don't know and figuring out the best next step for learning them are key to both getting experience and finding a job.

Summary

In this chapter, you learned what type of job experience most employers look for when hiring a Salesforce consultant. You also learned how to volunteer for pro bono work to gain Salesforce experience if you do not have any. You also learned the types of recruiters and how to work with recruiters and how to use LinkedIn to find job postings.

Resources

Catch a Fire, https://www.catchafire.org/

Taproot Foundation, https://taprootfoundation.org/

Volunteer Match, https://www.volunteermatch.org/search/index.jsp

Points of Light Engage, https://engage.pointsoflight.org/

Idealist, https://www.idealist.org

Preparing for a Software Project

The Evolution of Software Development

The process of creating software has gone through several significant incarnations that are important to understand if you want to advise clients on the best way to develop software. The activity of writing software for computers began in the middle of the 20th century using tools and techniques that would be unfamiliar to most people today. Automation led to digital modernization strategies with priorities from companies to make changes to software more and more often. Newer project management methodologies such as Agile and Scrum incorporated the concept of continuous feedback to accommodate the pace of change. The software development lifecycle emerged as the need to create efficiency around the process of creating software intensified. At first, project management methodologies such as Waterfall were sufficient, but gradually other methodologies emerged to keep up with the accelerating need for software changes.

© Heather Negley 2022
H. Negley, *The Salesforce Consultant's Guide*,
https://doi.org/10.1007/978-1-4842-7960-1_4

Software development started in the 1950s, and almost immediately engineers strove to find ways to make software faster.[1] Even as early as the beginning of the 19th century, people used rectangle cards with punched-out holes (Figure 4-1). These were called *punch cards*. Every line of a punch card had a couple of holes that were punched out in a certain area of the card. Depending on where the holes were on the card, they represented different characters that made up words or numbers.

Figure 4-1. Census worker with Hollerith pantograph punch. Source: Truesdell, Leon E., The Development of Punch Card Tabulation in the Bureau of the Census: 1890-1940, US GPO, 1965, page 144

IBM dominated the landscape of punch cards and machines in the 1960s and 1970s.[2] Punch card programming employed a method known as *structured programming*. The disadvantage of this type of programming is when changes have to be made to a program, the corresponding changes have to be made in each place in the program that effects that change. This can be a very time-consuming process if the program is large.

The need to change software programs often has only increased as time has gone on and the speed at which we communicate has increased. From landline phones to email to texting to social media, communication is faster than ever.

Automation

A lot of Salesforce projects support digital modernization strategies. Companies are under pressure to digitize their services and to automate their processes.[3] As a Salesforce consultant, it is important to know how to best

---

[1] CS302: Jared King's "The History of Software." learn.saylor.org. Retrieved 04-06-2021.
[2] "The IBM Punched Card." Retrieved on 04-06-2021 from: http://www-03.ibm.com/ibm/history/ibm100/us/en/icons/punchcard/
[3] Afshar, Vala, Top 8 trends shaping digital transformation in 2021, https://www.zdnet.com/article/top-8-trends-shaping-digital-transformation-in-2021/

support employees who are going through these types of changes. Jobs may change from paper based, and new skills need to be learned. Tasks that automation cannot replace can be viewed as tasks that complement the automated tasks.[4] For example, rote repetition from software and creativity from a person are where humans and machines work together. They work hand in hand to achieve goals not against each other. We still need humans to do skills that require flexibility, judgment, creativity, and common sense.[5] Automation replaces routine jobs that can be codified. Rote tasks can be codified, which saves time, and humans can work on the higher-order thinking that they are better at doing. For example, Bloom's taxonomy of thinking skills includes application, analysis, synthesis, evaluation, and creation.[6] These are all skills in which humans excel. These concepts may be new ways of thinking about technology for your clients, but it is important that you take the time to educate them if you see a need.

If you have a client who is worried that automation will replace their job, looking to the lessons of the past is helpful. In the beginning of the 19th century, agriculture was the dominant industry. Then the automobile was invented, and machines substituted manpower. There was no longer a need for blacksmiths, but there was a need for car mechanics. While some jobs became obsolete, other things like gas stations were born. Technology did not eliminate jobs in the long term, but jobs changed. In another example from the 1980s, ATMs did not replace bank tellers. The number of banks rose, but the number of bank tellers per branch fell. Bank tellers became more involved in relationship banking.

As a Salesforce consultant, you may encounter people who think that their jobs may be eliminated due to automation, and they worry there won't be enough new jobs to replace the old ones. But this concern has been around for a long time. In the 1950s, Lyndon Johnson created the Blue-Ribbon National Commission on Technology, Automation, and Economic Progress to study this problem. Their final conclusion was that automation did not lead to a decline in jobs.[7] Automation does change the types of jobs that are needed. Certain jobs may become obsolete, but there is plenty of new work. In other words, automation complements output, which in turn leads to more labor. Computers substitute for workers in routine tasks while amplifying the need for people to do problem solving and creativity-based jobs. And the tacit

---

[4] Journal of Economic Perspectives, https://pubs.aeaweb.org/doi/pdfplus/10.1257/jep.29.3.3
[5] ibid. p. 3
[6] Higher Order Thinking: Bloom's Taxonomy, https://learningcenter.unc.edu/tips-and-tools/higher-order-thinking/
[7] Journal of Economic Perspectives, https://pubs.aeaweb.org/doi/pdfplus/10.1257/jep.29.3.3

knowledge that people have is very powerful when coupled with the knowledge that an automated system produces. Being open to change and open to learning new skills is the right mindset to have. Change happens more often than it used to, and being adaptable is important.

Software Development Lifecycle

In the 1960s, the software development lifecycle (SDLC) emerged as a framework to plan, implement, test, document, deploy, and maintain software. It started as the "systems development lifecycle" to help businesses manage their systems.[8] A software framework is a way to logically organize the activities around creating an application into a standard process that is repeatable no matter the type of software. This guidebook covers two major types of project management methodologies, Waterfall and Agile, that complement the SDCL framework, since these are the ones you will most likely encounter on a Salesforce project. There are several adaptations of Agile. Scrum[9] is one example and one that you may hear about on Salesforce projects. Many consulting firms create their own proprietary methodologies to suit their business needs. Sometimes teams refer to their methodologies as "semi-agile" or "wagile," meaning a combination of Agile and Waterfall. The reason that they spend the time and effort doing this is to take the parts of the methodologies that they like and combine them into something new to suit their services or product.

Waterfall

Waterfall is a sequential way to create a piece of software. Each step is followed one step after the next in a linear fashion until the application is complete. Like structured programming, it is also time-consuming to make changes with the Waterfall approach, and clients often change their mind about what they want.[10] Also, if there is a misalignment between what the clients want and what the developers build, then the time to complete can drastically increase.

I have seen clients change their minds over and again about what they want. It is a common occurrence in the evolution of an application and is expected behavior. A client usually doesn't know exactly what they want, but they know

---

[8] Elliott, G. (2004). Global Business Information Technology: An Integrated Systems Approach. United Kingdom: Pearson Addison Wesley.
[9] https://www.scrum.org/resources/what-is-scrum
[10] Bogdan-Alexandru ANDREI, "A Study on Using Waterfall and Agile Methods in Software Project Management." Journal of Information Systems & Operations Management, www.rebe.rau.ro/RePEc/rau/jisomg/SU19/JISOM-SU19-A12.pdf

what they like when they see it, and it sparks their curiosity, and they can envision the next evolution. However, they can often get ahead of themselves and ask for full-blown automation right away.

For example, a client may be refactoring their manual paper process to process automation with approval processes and data migrations. Salesforce advises a Crawl, Walk, Run approach to regulate this very behavior.[11] While it is exciting to see a client envision their future, a consultant must be able to be a guide and lead the way to get there in a responsible manner. The Crawl, Walk, Run approach can be applied to any project. In the example with a manual paper process, crawling may consist of getting the information into Salesforce and setting up the fields, Walking may consist of creating approval processes and other automation, and running may consist of creating a near real-time data integration.

Figure 4-2 shows the structure of a Waterfall project. A Waterfall project starts with the client business users or their representatives explaining what they would like for their software to do to the project team. These are the requirements, and they can consist of describing a software that they currently have and what they like and don't like about it. There may be a demo of the current software. They may talk about the business processes that they have. The development team writes the requirements and then designs a solution for the client. Then they develop the software and test it and then give it back to the client.

Figure 4-2. Waterfall

---

[11] Kathy Koh-Gigant, *Crawl, Walk, Run: A Guide to Salesforce Implementation*, https://www.salesforce.org/blog/crawl-walk-run-salesforce-implementation-guide/

Acceleration of Change

The software development lifecycle has significantly accelerated in the 21st century. This means the amount of time that used to be acceptable to develop a piece of software is no longer acceptable. Waterfall development is a style of development that is left over from this slower era. As you just learned, in Waterfall *all* requirements are gathered and written before a single piece of code is written. Then at the end of the project, the client finally gets to see the finished product. In Agile, the development phase cycles through sprints that are a short amount of time for planning, development, and feedback. This creates iterative development. An agile project has more than one sprint. Generally, if a project has one sprint, then it is considered a Waterfall project.

Agile

Agile is a class of methodologies that is used to organize and manage complex software development projects. In 2001, 17 software developers created the Agile Manifesto, which established the values around this approach. The elegance of Agile is that it is flexible enough for any team to adopt. Emphasis is placed on individuals over processes, working software over comprehensive documentation, client collaboration over contract language, and nimbly responding to change instead of following a plan.[12] Scrum is a popular type of Agile. There are several others such as Kanban, Extreme Programming, and Feature-Driven Development.

Agile projects have a backlog, which is a list of items that need to be done on a project.[13] A project backlog is a list of user stories that are written from the end-user point of view such as a salesperson or a customer service person. The user stories describe what the person would like to do in their process. These stories are written so they are independent of technology or a solution.

Unique roles on an Agile project using Scrum include scrum master and product owner. Scrum masters help teams apply the rules of Agile. This is a different role than project managers, who have different responsibilities. There is more on this distinction in responsibilities in Chapter 5. The scrum master protects the team and helps resolve obstacles to problems. They do not make decisions on the software solution itself. They are more of a guide or a coach. The product owner decides which features should be built first. Oftentimes this role is found on the client side.

---

[12] The Agile Manifesto, https://agilemanifesto.org/
[13] Bogdan-Alexandru ANDREI, "A Study on Using Waterfall and Agile Methods in Software Project Management." *Journal of Information Systems & Operations Management*, http://www.rebe.rau.ro/RePEc/rau/jisomg/SU19/JISOM-SU19-A12.pdf, p.127

Sprinting

The biggest difference between Agile and Waterfall is the concept of sprints. Sprints are a time-boxed unit of time for which a predetermined amount of work is performed. For example, a project could have a sprint that lasts two weeks. This means the development team would work on a specific amount of work for those two weeks. During that time they will attend Agile ceremonies or meetings to help move the sprint along.

At the end of a sprint, a team might go right into another sprint called sprint 2. And this can go on and on. I once joined a project during its 16th sprint. It ended at 17, which was more than enough for that project. The team had been sprinting for 10 months straight, and it was time to release the software.

Another key difference that sets Agile projects apart from Waterfall are the timing of demos. In Agile, demos are held at the end of each sprint. It is during the demo that a developer invites the client to a meeting and shows them the little bit of work that they have been doing. Then the client tells the development team their initial impressions. This is the heart of continuous feedback and iteration (Figure 4-3). The team tweaks their work, adjusts their user story, refines the functionality, and shows the client the work again at the next demo. Then the team can move on to another piece of functionality. In Waterfall projects, demos occur at the end of development. If ambiguities arise and clarifying questions need to be made, then this isn't the most efficient approach and can cause rework, which impacts the time and cost of the project. Waterfall can work fine if the project is small.[14] A small team can most likely manage the solution and scope for a short timeline.

Figure 4-3. Agile is based on cycles of iterative development driven by continuous feedback

---

[14] ibid. p.127

The Value of Continuous Feedback

The problem with Waterfall development is illustrated in the famous cartoon shown in Figure 4-4. The client asked for a tire swing. Each box illustrates how different members of the team interpreted that request. In the first box, the client explains what is a "tier swing" for some reason. Maybe it was their accent, who knows! Miscommunication happens quickly and easily. So from the very beginning, the tire is left out of the requirements. But as you can see from box 12, what they need is a tire swing.

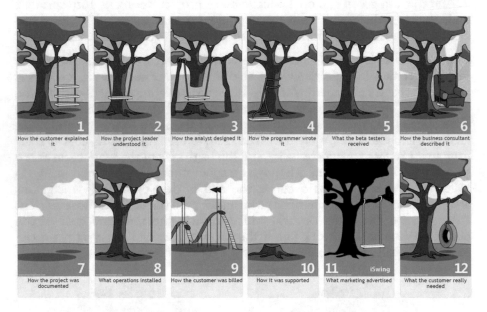

Figure 4-4. Tree Swing picture. Source: Adapted from Mirai, Michi, Project Management - A Tree Swing Story, ZenTao, July 11, 2020, https://www.zentao.pm/agile-knowledge-share/tree-swing-project-management-cartoon-97.mhtml, image source: https://urldefense.com/v3/__http://www.projectcartoon.com/cartoon/11111

The second box shows that the project leader understood that the client wanted a swing but probably didn't understand what "tier" meant so just interpreted the request as a swing. If he had asked the client to repeat what they said or repeated back what he heard then, this could have been avoided. Requirements gathering is an important first step in a project, and communication should be fluid like the type that is found in a conversation. See more on communication techniques in Chapter 11.

The third box illustrates a funny/not funny outcome that can happen if an analyst over-engineers business requirements and doesn't incorporate a solution design to illustrate what is possible. The product is impossible to build in real life as the requirements are written. This is a common occurrence, and it is easy to blame the client if you are working in a vacuum. Feedback at this point would have helped get the project back on track. But instead, the developer built what was possible (fourth box). The code did include key elements such as the two ropes looped around a tree. There was probably no acceptance criteria because the product is still not usable and not testable (fifth box), and there was no process or accountability from anyone on the team for writing documentation (seventh box). The fourth box illustrates that programmers often have no context and just build what they are asked to build without thinking about the big picture. To give developers some credit here, oftentimes they are not told what the big picture is and what the client actually wants to do with the product and are not invited to client-facing meetings.

This cartoon also illustrates the work that goes into making a product. Marketing (11th box) actually took the time to make a snazzy, slick sheet before the client even saw a mockup of the design because there was no design. Remarkably operations got the closest to what the client really wanted, but it was incomplete. They barely got started but probably thought they were done. This is something a demo with the client could have easily remedied. They would have said this is not a minimum viable product. It is a rope hanging from a tree, not a swing. It also shows the disconnect between developers and operations. Handoffs are important so that everyone aligns on expectation, assumptions, design, and process. More on this in Chapter 6. All in all, the client paid a lot of money (ninth box) for something they didn't even want, and they probably decided they didn't want to work with the consultant again because they were out of money (ninth box). The consultant over-promised (sixth box) and failed to deliver (eighth box). Had refinements, continuous feedback, and course corrections been done early and throughout the project, it would have saved time money and the end result would have aligned to the actual vision.

Summary

Software has evolved over time as the pace of change has accelerated. As technological innovations have given way to more efficient machines, software has played a big role in automating systems and processes. Humans who once had to perform rote tasks can hand off these activities to software much in the same way they handed off muscle power to machines. Software frameworks have evolved to accommodate a world where the need for change is ubiquitous. It is important to teach your clients the evanescent lessons of past technology transformation such as from horse to car so they can think in analogous terms about their present challenges. And providing soliciting continuous feedback during the software project is a powerful technique that little by little will shape and align the application to the client vision.

Resources

- Punch Card Programming, Computerphile, `https://youtu.be/KG2M4ttzBnY`; professor Brailsford describes the mechanics of a stack of punch card from the 1970s

- Bubbles Whiting, *Using Punch Cards, Hollerith and IBM, The Center for Computing History*, `https://youtu.be/L7jAOcc9kBU`

- The Agile Manifesto, `https://agilemanifesto.org/`

Common Project Roles

When you work on a Salesforce project, you can be a functional or technical consultant. A role is a specific job. Functional roles include project management and roles that directly interface with the client. Technical roles include developer and architect, but there is overlap, and oftentimes these roles also interact with the client. Usually, the interaction is more about the solution and not the terms of the contract. There are many resources created by successful Salesforce professionals that can be useful to reference depending on your role.

What Is a Consultant?

I met Behzad Habibzai in 2015 when I was working for an up-and-coming systems integrator, a Salesforce partner. Behzad was the Salesforce administrator for the partner firm, but as I later learned is also an accomplished flamenco guitar player.[1] He had a warm, outgoing personality when I told him how important I thought his role was to a company full of Salesforce consultants. As the years went by, Behzad and I kept in touch and had the chance to work together again when he became a consultant for another firm

---

[1] https://www.behzadhabibzai.com/

© Heather Negley 2022
H. Negley, *The Salesforce Consultant's Guide*,
https://doi.org/10.1007/978-1-4842-7960-1_5

where I worked. He helped on both the admin side and as a consultant, eventually making the switch to a full-time consultant. He has worked in the ecosystem for nine years now and has eight certifications, but he has accumulated them at a pace of about one a year, which I have always thought was a smart and manageable way to go about it. He prides himself on his breadth of Salesforce knowledge from the Sales, Service, Experience, and Education clouds as well as in automation, reporting, data migration, and AppExchange products. He even dabbles in Apex (coding) from time to time. I think Behzad is a good example of a consultant who approaches Salesforce consulting in a smart and manageable way. It's not a race. It's a journey full of growth and learning that collects. This approach will give you the flexibility to have a balanced life with time to hone your passions and talents both in your career and in life outside of work.

Consulting experience takes time to accumulate in order to turn you into an expert who advises. No matter your role, your experiences pile up over time. Each project you complete gives you a new layer of knowledge. No two projects are alike, so the more projects you experience, the more dynamic your wisdom becomes. When you work on a Salesforce project, think of each person on the project team as a consultant. It is the job of the team to give the client the best implementation journey and act as a trusted adviser who guides the client to the solution that meets their goals. Client goals often come from their strategic plan. They may have key performance indicators (KPIs) that are tied to a strategic goal and are measurable. Salesforce is often seen as a tool that can be used to help reach and measure these goals. See Chapter 8 for more on how to use KPIs to shape a solution.

The job function that a consultant takes on in a project is called a *role*. Each consultant on the team is assigned a role. Roles are assigned to a project based on the scope of work and have different areas of skill specialization. Consultants may also switch roles from one project to the next, but they are still considered consultants. On agile projects, this is seen as a strength, because they can act as backups for their teammates. This type of redundancy makes a project team stronger. Each role has a distinct set of activities and responsibilities that can vary from project to project. As long as everyone on the team knows what the roles and responsibilities are and what the crossover tasks are, then the team will be healthy and productive. See Chapter 7 on project preparation and knowing your role.

When you are just starting out and are not sure what type of role that you want to specialize in, I suggest having an open mind to project roles. If you see yourself as a consultant first and the project as a new experience, there is less of a reason to get hung up on the role. Also, if you see the roles not in terms of who has the most perceived power but more as a team of people working together, then the role you choose should not matter as much. Power and influence can come from any role on the team and are separate from doing the work. Wisdom accumulates with experience, so consultants advise on knowledge gained from past projects, and that should really be your goal: to gain as much experience and knowledge as possible.

What Is the Difference Between Functional and Technical Roles?

To be an effective Salesforce consultant, you need to have a mix of both functional and technical skills. Functional skills are soft consulting skills like communication, emotional intelligence, critical thinking, and client management. Part III of this book goes over these key functional skills in detail. The remainder of this chapter explains the technical and functional roles with references to resources to acquire more specific skills.

Sometimes you run across people who are part technical and part functional. This is an important skill because they serve as a bridge between the technical work and the vision and strategy. They have the ability to translate business language into technical language and are often very strong communicators who know how to properly use analogies to help people understand each other. Similar to a translator between two languages, they translate between technical speak and business speak. Every business has its own set of jargon and acronyms. Technofunctional people are very good at learning new business jargon quickly.

For example, a technofunctional person may find themselves trying to explain the concept of an object to a client who works on the business side. They may have to do this because the client business user is asking for a change at the end of the project that will require a data model change. Using technical language with the business user will not work. The ability to translate in this case comes in handy. Here the consultant might say, "The change you are asking for is as complex as adding a new room to the middle of a house after it has already been built and wired with electricity. We could do it, but we are going to have to undo a lot of other stuff, and it will cost more time and money to do. Perhaps there is a better alternative that we can discuss or we can plan this for the future."

Conversely, a technofunctional consultant may have to explain the big picture to a developer who has spent too much time on the details of a solution. For example, if a client is going from a paper-based system to a workflow automated system, they may not need to create complex logical triggers on edge case scenarios before they have gotten used to the new job processes that the database creates. Their efficiency will sky rocket with a minimal first-step solution, and they may not even be aware of the time they will save or completely understand how they want the app to evolve until they have spent some time getting used to it. In this example, the technofunctional consultant should explain the big picture to the developer consultant using analogies again. For example, Salesforce has a term it recommends using for this common scenario called "Crawl, Walk, Run." Salesforce advises consultants to tell clients to crawl first with a minimum viable product and then ease into full-blown automation. It is more of an evolutionary approach. So, the technofunctional consultant would tell the developer, "This client is in the crawl phase of Crawl, Walk, Run. They don't need complex triggers, and status changes should be mostly manual until we get to walking, which isn't on the roadmap for at least six months when we start doing the integration."

Developers can build really cool apps, but they can also build apps that are overly complex and can become unusable to the end user, as we saw in the previous chapter with the swing example. That's why the technofunctional role is so critical.

To put a fine point on this, in this example, if the project manager is purely functional and the developer is purely technical, they may fail to communicate what the client really needs. Remember in Figure 4-4, the last square is what the client really needs. "What does the client want?" is one of the most important questions that a Salesforce consultant has to keep asking themselves during a project, and if no one on your project is doing that, it is a big risk. My advice is if you want to bring the most value to a team, then be the person who reminds everyone of the big picture at critical times. Yes, sometimes even the obvious can be overlooked. This is why technofunctional roles are so important. They are the people who remind us why we are all here.

Roles

A role is your job title on a project. It is important to distinguish this from your job title for the company that you work for. If you are a consultant, you probably work for a consulting firm. This is the company that pays you. If you work for a consulting firm, your title might be Consultant, Senior Consultant, Manager, or Director. These titles are general and have more to do with your level of consulting experience, which is what the consulting firm is concerned about. The consulting firm uses this leveling to determine how much to charge the client for your services.

If you are working for a reputable firm, then you have opportunities to interact with other consultants to share and learn about different project experiences and career timelines. You may find mentors this way, especially after you decide on a specialty. Technologies change all the time. Some consulting firms don't specialize in Salesforce but in a lot of technologies. But there are also smaller firms or boutique firms that do. But if a technology gets big enough like Salesforce has, then the bigger consulting firms will create practices dedicated to one technology.

The next section explains the most common roles that you will find on a Salesforce project. This is not an exhaustive list. It is based on my experience and is what I have observed from dozens of projects and the hundreds of other Salesforce consultants I have met along the way.

Project Managers, Scrum Masters

Project managers and scrum masters are functional roles in charge of managing a project. Project managers initiate, plan, execute, monitor, and close projects. They follow a project management framework with their own set of tools and methods depending on the type of project. They often have the Project Management Professional (PMP) certification issued by the Project Management Institute. Scrum masters are certified by the Scrum Alliance and are a type of project manager who is trained to manage Agile projects.

There are three major constraints that project managers use to balance projects. They are scope, schedule, and cost (see Figure 5-1). Project managers are constantly trying to maintain equilibrium between these three constraints throughout the life of a project. They also manage risks and issues as methods to help keep the three constraints balanced.

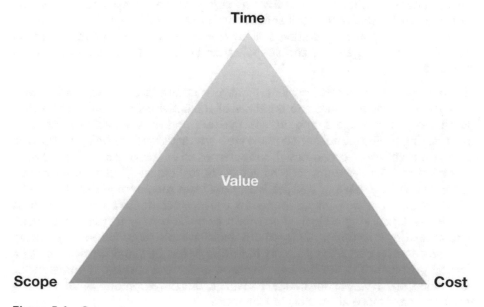

Figure 5-1. Constraints

The scope of a project defines the breadth and depth of the work. Scope is derived from the statement of work or contract. The team breaks down the scope into workable pieces called a *work breakdown structure*. At the beginning of a project, the team holds a series of meetings called *discovery* and asks the client detailed questions about the project scope. (See Chapter 8 for more on discovery.) The output of these meetings are the written requirements or user stories for Agile projects. These requirements help the project manager manage the scope of the work and create traceability as the project progresses into the testing phase.

Project managers use an industry-standard method for measuring the financial progress of a project and forecasting future work; it's called *earned-value analysis* (EVA). A time and materials contract in which a consultant's time is billed by the hour is an example of a situation where EVA is a critical tool for measuring if the project is over or under budget. Some projects are sold for a fixed-price lump sum. For these projects, managing scope creep becomes critical. Scope creep occurs when the client asks for little changes that are beyond the scope of the contract. Usually, project teams are inclined to make small changes that take less than 15 minutes because they want to help and find it difficult to say no to something so simple, but these types of requests are a slippery slope and can quickly get out of control and evolve into something else entirely. Properly managing scope creep and having the communication skills set to tell a client "no" in a straightforward yet diplomatic way is an important consulting skill to learn. See Chapter 12 for more on scope creep management, and see Chapter 11 for more on communication techniques.

To manage the timeline, project managers create project schedules with activity lists that measure the duration of the activities as well as the costs. Both project managers and scrum masters spend a great deal of time monitoring project timelines to make sure that activities are being completed by team members. Sometimes this is referred to as "driving a project toward completion." Activities sometimes get stuck or "blocked," as scrum masters often say. A large part of this job is to help team members get unblocked by clearing away various impediments so the project doesn't churn and miss deadlines. Unsticking a blocked activity may mean turning a risk into an issue and escalating it to upper management decision-makers, or it could also mean bringing two experts together to have a conversation and work through a logical problem to make the best decision under the current circumstances. On Agile projects, scrum masters manage the development timeline using sprints. Learn more about this in Chapter 9.

Business Analyst, Business Architect

Business analysts manage the requirements and capabilities in a project. They write user stories and create process flows that map out the client's business processes. They usually start their work during discovery where they lead the business users through a series of questions to map out their processes. If the project involves business project reengineering, which a lot of Salesforce projects do, then the business analyst will map out the current business processes or current state and then work with the business stakeholders to determine where they need improvement to arrive at a future state. On Salesforce projects, it is common for people in this role to also do the configuration in the Salesforce org. Configuration is point-and-click work. This means setting up the back-end system by clicking fields on or off. I am simplifying it a little because it can be quite complicated to know which setting to configure, but the main point is that it does not involve writing lines of code. You may have seen promotions from Salesforce that say "clicks not code." I've even seen the software industry as a whole refer to this concept as "low code, no code." In both cases, they are referring to configuration interfaces.

A business architect is a strategic job who analyzes business processes across business units. They focus on improving business operations to align with goals and strategy. They often use a method called *roadmapping*, which is a way to plan for changes over a long period of time.

Solution Architect

Solution architects analyze the requirements, process flows, and any other work products created by the business analyst. They also work closely with project managers to understand the balance of the three critical constraints of the project. As you learned in the previous section, these are cost, time, and scope. They study the project management plan, risks and issues, and any other pertinent information to determine the best technical path forward. The work products from other team members serve as inputs for solution architects to use creativity and logic to design and architect solutions that solve technical problems so that the complexity of the architecture is kept to a minimum and overengineering is avoided.

For example, sometimes stakeholders ask for functionality that is beyond the capabilities of point-and-click configuration and requires custom development to complete. But the project might be constrained by a tight budget that cannot be exceeded even through a change order. The impact to the solution is that there is no flexibility for custom development. More development time increases the cost. Custom development involves working with Apex code and takes more time than configuration changes in a Salesforce org.

Apex is a strongly typed, object-oriented programming language developed by Salesforce. It works on the Lightning platform server by allowing developers to execute flow and transaction control statements in conjunction with calls to the Lightning Platform API. The solution architect may also have conversations or "solutioning" sessions to help the stakeholder make decisions. Solutioning should never start before all the requirements are collected. Team members may talk through various options for the project, but it is the solution architect's responsibility to create the solution.

Change Manager, Trainer

The change manager is the role in charge of user adoption and training. Sometimes this role is split into two roles, change manager and trainer. Change managers commonly receive certifications from an organization named Prosci, which has a professional training program and change management certification program that teaches students how to use their Adkar methodology. Adkar is an acronym that stands for Awareness, Desire, Knowledge, Ability, and Reinforcement and is designed to lead organizations through change.

Change managers work with the stakeholders to identify influencers to help craft a vision for change as well as a plan to execute the change throughout the company. They collaborate to develop socialization strategies that fit within the culture of the organization and then execute on methods to bring about user adoption and reinforcement. For example, the change manager may develop a communication schedule that lists the types of communication methods that will be used to communicate with different audiences in a company. Examples are town halls for company-wide announcements or email newsletters for weekly updates to the project team and stakeholders. Change managers also work closely with the scrum team to document changes to the current stakeholder process to understand the types of changes being made and who they will impact. This work product serves as an input to the training curriculum.

The trainer creates a curriculum for the end-user training that is based on the work that the development team is completing. For example, if a project has six sprints, the trainer may work a sprint behind the development team to create the training materials for the features and functionality that has already been completed and accepted. The trainer leads classes at various intervals both for end users as well as for Salesforce administrators. The classes focus on the implementation and rarely are Salesforce training classes. If the students are new to Salesforce, the trainer will often recommend pertinent trailhead modules or outside classes as a supplement.

When project teams are small, the training activities are picked up by other roles on the project such as project manager, business analysts, or solution architect. It is common for the team to hold a session called Train the Trainer that is intended to teach a few stakeholders the implementation so that they can hold their own internal training classes. This helps keep project costs down for the client. It is also common to hold administrator training using this same small team format to teach the client administrator about the new changes that were made during the implementation so they can properly maintain the system for the end users.

Certified Technical Architect

The certified technical architect (CTA) role overlaps with the developer and data architect roles and depending on the skill level of the person even the solution architect role. This is a high-level technical role that plans the architecture of the systems that are needed to maintain an enterprise-wide digital initiative or a large-scale Salesforce deployment. CTAs know how to adhere to analysis, design, and development standards. This role is knowledgeable about integration points and related implementation architecture for business usage improvements, scalability, and performance. For example, a CTA will often have many of the skills that are expected from data analysts, developers, and solution architects such as integrating Salesforce with other applications, synchronizing Salesforce with external systems and data sources, or even knowing when and how to use process flows, triggers, sharing, data, visibility, and security.

The certification path to attain the CTA designation is not easy. It takes at least two to three years if not longer to achieve. There are numerous certifications needed as prerequisites, and then applicants are required to sit for a review board exam.[2] This certification is so difficult that the number of people with the certification is only in the hundreds.[3] On the other hand, the salaries for this role are some of the highest in the Salesforce ecosystem from USD $136,515 for a junior level to USD $167,466 for the senior level.[4]

---

[2] Salesforce Architect Journeys, https://trailhead.salesforce.com/credentials/architectoverview
[3] Becoming a Salesforce Certified Technical Architect – Thoughts From 9 CTAs, Retrieved May 18, 2021, https://www.salesforceben.com/become-a-salesforce-certified-technical-architect/
[4] Salesforce Technical Architect Salary, Mason Frank International, Retrieved May 26, 2021, https://www.masonfrank.com/salesforce-salary-survey/salesforce-technical-architect-salary

Also, a new industry of CTA coaches has emerged to support candidates through this process. Flow Republic (https://flowrepublic.com/) is one such company. It offers CTA coaching to help candidates study for the CTA as well as a communication bootcamp that is intended to help introverts struggling to speak effectively.

Many technical architects have not finished all the certification requirements but are still quite knowledgeable and bring tremendous value to projects.

Data Architect

A data architect is a technical role. They work with clients to help turn their data into knowledge that solves business problems. Sometimes this means the data architect plans and creates data models showing the relationships between data tables or objects and fields. Other times, the data architect advises on how to connect and move data from one place to another in a secure way. This is referred to as a *data migration*. An integration, a subcategory of a migration, is a way to combine data from two different sources to give users a unified view of them and is also a common component of a Salesforce implementation for which this role is responsible.

Highly skilled people in this role may do everything from data migrations and integrations to data mappings and transforming data using ETL tools and connectors. ETL is shorthand for extract, transform, load, the common data process of copying data from one place and making it fit into the context of the new place. Data mappings are part of the transformation work to map fields to one another sometimes by creating rules to do this. Salesforce has a data import tool that comes with the platform called Dataloader.io, but sometimes clients have licenses to more robust ETL tools such as Informatica, and those may be utilized for data transformation work.

A skilled Salesforce data architect will also understand how Salesforce's data theory is different from traditional relational databases and their normalization rules. They will understand the trade-offs that Salesforce made to the platform for speed and limitations with SOQL, which is Salesforce's version of SQL.[5] SQL stands for structured query language and is a language used to access and manipulate data from databases.

In 2019, Salesforce acquired a powerful analytical platform called Tableau. This acquisition significantly extends the analytical capability of the Salesforce. Tableau has drag-and-drop visual analysis that makes creating data visualizations fast. Tableau has a separate certification program, community group, and learning program, although Trailhead does have quite a few Tableau modules.

---

[5] Masri, David, Developing Data Migrations and Integrations with Salesforce, p.13–35, https://www.apress.com/gp/book/9781484242087

There is also a popular role called a data visualization specialist who specializes in creating data visualizations from multiple sources of useful information. These visualizations can help clients make decisions. For example, data visualization specialists may utilize analytical and visualization tools to aggregate geographic, demographic, military, and academic data to design and deliver an infographic on what it takes to become a NASA astronaut and put it on Tableau Public to share in a public space. (See Figure 5-2.)[6]

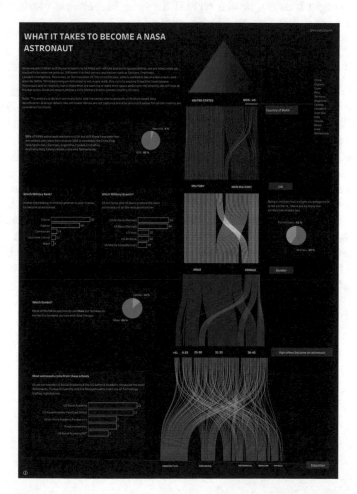

Figure 5-2. Visualization (Source: Kumar, Vinodh, What Does It Take to Become a NASA Astronaut, Tableau Public, retrieved on May 27, 2021, https://public.tableau.com/en-us/gallery/what-does-take-become-nasa-astronaut?tab=viz-of-the-day&type=viz-of-the-day)

---

[6] What Does It Take to Become a NASA Astronaut, Retrieved on May 27, 2021, https://public.tableau.com/en-us/gallery/what-does-take-become-nasa-astronaut?tab=viz-of-the-day&type=viz-of-the-day

Developer

There is a high demand for developers, so if this is the role you chose, you will have many opportunities. A Salesforce developer is skilled in the proprietary coding language owned by Salesforce called Apex, which is similar to Java. Developers write code to extend the platform when point-and-click configuration is not enough to implement a solution. Salesforce also created Visualforce pages that are similar to HTML pages. HyperText Markup Language (HTML) is a basic foundation of web pages.

Women in Programming

If you think programming is just for men, think again. In fact, the first computer programmer was a woman. Her name was Ada Lovelace (Figure 5-3), and she was a mathematician born in 1815. She studied both music and math and was way ahead of her time. She created the first algorithm, or series of instructions for Charles Babbage's mechanical computer idea called the Analytical Engine, which would calculate Bernoulli numbers. Bernoulli numbers are a sequence of numbers used to find formulas. She is seen as a visionary for her ideas and statement that the machine "might act upon other things besides number... the Engine might compose elaborate and scientific pieces of music of any degree of complexity or extent."[7] She realized that symbols could be manipulated by the machine instead of just numbers. Ada's legacy is still with us today. The cryptocurrency ADA for the public blockchain platform Cardono is named after her.[8]

---

[7] Computer History Museum, https://www.computerhistory.org/babbage/adalovelace/, Retrieved May 28, 2021
[8] What is ADA?, https://cardano.org/what-is-ada/, Retrieved May 28, 2021

Figure 5-3. Portrait of Ada Lovelace at age 20 (Source: New York Public Library, `https://digitalcollections.nypl.org/items/8562182e-4845-db2b-e040-e00a18060ea6`)

A more modern female developer is Kiran Jaescon, who began Women Code Heroes. Kiran wanted to give back to her community after being inspired by a local community program that her employer was involved in that taught rural families about computers. Kiran noticed that a lot of women get stuck as administrators who did not even realize what they were missing in development work. Kiran also noticed that there is a barrier to entry for some reason and wanted to do something about it. She is also one of the cofounders of RAD Woman.[9]

RAD (`http://radwomen.org/`) stands for Radical Apex Developers and provides a supportive and collaborative environment for female Salesforce administrators to learn Apex. According to the National Center for Women & Information Technology, 25 percent of technology workers are women, and this number has been declining since 1991 when it reached a high of 36 percent. If you look at the category of software developers, the percentage falls to just 18 percent. Female patenting is very low at only 2 percent for female-only teams.[10] RAD holds free developer classes for women who have two years of Salesforce experience but have never coded.

---

[9] `http://womencodeheroes.com/about-me/`
[10] Ashcraft, Catherine, Women in Tech: The Facts, p2

I once had the experience of listening to a CEO opine about how he thought he only had the option to take stay-at-home moms and make them Salesforce administrators but not consultants, which is what he really needed. Despite my protests, he remained unconvinced. This limiting belief surely does not help women feel unstuck. Luckily, there are forward-thinking women like Kiran Jaescon and also Gemma Blezard who have vision and are blazing new trails.

Gemma Blezard founded Ladies Be Architects (https://ladies-be-architects.com) as a community initiative with a mission to grow the number of female Salesforce-certified technical architects, which like developers is also currently an underrepresented population. Ladies Be Architect holds virtual study groups where students can ask questions on various topics such as sharing and visibility, fundamentals of data modeling, and more. You can also watch the previous study groups as well on their website (https://ladies-be-architects.com/category/study-groups/planned-study-groups).

Women Code Heros (http://womencodeheroes.com/) is Kiran Jaescon's site. The Resources and Learning to Code sections have a lot of useful information on basic coding principles using cooking metaphors, which makes the concepts easier to understand for new learners.

Quality Assurance Engineer

Quality assurance (QA) or testing is an important part of any project. The ability to write comprehensive test scripts is oftentimes critical to project success and helps to create traceability to prevent scope creep. Test scripts are a set of instructions used to test a piece of functionality to make sure it functions as expected. Advanced QA engineers know how to write automated test scripts. Sometimes teams use behavior-driven development to test software. Business analysts will write their user stories in gherkin syntax (see Chapter 8), and then QA engineers will write their test scripts in Cucumber, which is an input into automated testing. Selenium is a technology used to run these types of test scripts. At this level, this role requires a technical skill set. On the other hand, functional QAs are good at finding defects in configurations and testing the system overall to uncover edge cases and other potential problems simply by testing the system as a test user.

It cannot be overstated how important testing is in software development. Sometimes teams have a tendency to rush to the finish without thorough testing. Having a dedicated QA expert on the team is key. QA may not be for everyone, but some of the best Salesforce consultants that I have met have been people who have focused on QA.

More on Cucumber

Wynne, Matt, & Askak Hellesoy, Steve Tooke, *The Cucumber Book: Behaviour-Driven Development for Testers and Developers 2nd Edition*, https://www.amazon.com/Cucumber-Book-Behaviour-Driven-Development-Developers-dp-1680502387/dp/1680502387/ref=dp_ob_title_bk

Role-Based Resources

Many people who are at the top of their Salesforce careers have created resources and services for others. Here are a few recommendations from this talented group.

The *Salesforce Way* (https://salesforceway.com/podcast/) podcast is refreshing, well organized, and easy to listen to. It is hosted by Xi Xiao who interviews different experts from the Salesforce ecosystem. *Salesforce Way* doesn't try to be too many things, which makes it very consumable for someone visiting the site. Xi is also a good interviewer and asks questions that help listeners understand concepts that the guests are trying to explain.

The Joys of Apex (https://james.coding.blog/) is a blog written by James Simone. James is an interesting combination of writer and developer. His blog, which started as a tongue-and-cheek way for developers to bond over the limitations of the platform, has posts with names such as "The Tao of Apex" and "Lazy Interators." James was also a guest (https://salesforceway.com/podcast/dml-mocking-for-apex-test) on the *Salesforce Way* where he explained a DML mocking library that he created.

Automation Hour (http://www.automationhour.com), founded by Rakesh Gupta, Jennifer Lee, and David Litton, is a webinar held every other week that features a different special guest who presents on technical topics such as flows, which is declarative coding or point-and-click coding.

Jitendra Zaa writes an informative technical Salesforce blog (http://www.jitendrazaa.com/blog) that goes back to 2010.

Apex Hours (https://www.apexhours.com) is a content-rich resource with webinars from technical experts on topics such as data modeling, Apex triggers, Visualforce, platform events, Einstein next best actions, formulas, and admin life hacks (http://www.apexhours.com/formulas-and-admin-lifehacks/), to name a few.

Nanah Gregg's blog (https://nanahgregg.com) is a creative breath of fresh air. She communicates technical advice through analogy and quirky musings. For example, her hilarious but completely practical advice on org maintenance (https://nanahgregg.com/2021/02/25/salesforce-cleaning-menu-mild-a-flavor-for-everyone) is divided by the jalapeno levels of mild, medium, hot, and hell.

Summary

In this chapter, you learned that all the roles on a Salesforce project are consulting roles. You learned the difference between technical and functional roles as well as what the technofunctional role is and why it is an important role for a project team. You also learned about the special skills for some of the most common implementation roles including project manager and scrum manager who oversee time, scope, and budget, as well as client-facing roles such as business analyst, solution architect, change manager, and trainer. You also learned about more technical roles such as technical architect, data architect, and developer. You learned about specialized resources for women who may need help seeing a clear path into IT. You also learned more details about the training topics and areas of specialty for each role.

Resources

- Project Management Professional, https://www.pmi.org/certifications/project-management-pmp

- Patton, Jeff, User Story Mapping, https://www.jpattonassociates.com/user-story-mapping/

- The Prosci ADKAR® Model, https://www.prosci.com/adkar/adkar-model

- Developing Data Migrations and Integrations with Salesforce: Patterns and Best Practices, http://salesforcedatablog.com/#section-book

- Tableau Ambassador Program, https://www.tableau.com/community/community-leaders/ambassadors/apply

- Tableau Public, https://public.tableau.com

- Tableau Community, https://www.tableau.com/community

- Tableau Zen Masters, collection of selected community leaders, https://www.tableau.com/about/blog/2021/2/introducing-2021-tableau-zen-masters

- Tableau Role-Based Learning Paths, https://www.tableau.com/learn/learning-paths

- Tableau Certifications, https://www.tableau.com/learn/certification

- Salesforce offers a free developer edition (https://developer.salesforce.com/signup) for anyone who would like to test or practice using the platform. You might hear it referred to as a "developer org."

- Search the Force (https://searchtheforce.com) is a custom search engine created by Dan Applemen created to save research time. When you type a search term into the search box, a list of possible search terms pop up to help refine your search right away.

- Salesforce's site for architects, https://architect.salesforce.com/

Sales and Staffing

The activities before the sale of the project are called *presales*. The people in these roles are not considered consultants as they are not part of the implementation team; however, they are still part of the Ohana community. Some of them include contract review and resourcing planning, which you will learn more about in this chapter. Consultants are often involved in presales activities and can offer critical advice to set up a project for success. Once a project is sold, the account executive will hold a sales handoff meeting to explain the background of the project, as well as the scope, timeline, and budget. Sales handoffs are a good time for you to ask specific questions about the sales cycles so that you can learn about the personality of the client as well as other project expectations and assumptions.

Presales

The collection of activities before a project is sold is called *presales*. Presales start when someone in a sales role, such as an account executive, makes initial contact with a prospect; this is referred to as an *opportunity*. The meetings, phone calls, emails, and milestones are recorded in a customer relationship database (CRM) Sound familiar? Yes, it is nice when the consulting firm uses Salesforce as their CRM if you are a Salesforce consultant.

© Heather Negley 2022
H. Negley, *The Salesforce Consultant's Guide*,
https://doi.org/10.1007/978-1-4842-7960-1_6

The opportunity proceeds through a series of stages that ends once a sale is won or lost. Other stages may include the following:

- Business development, where the lead or prospect is determined to be qualified or not

- Initial contact with clients, such as writing proposals and other initial meetings

- Determining an appropriate approach

- Pitching and demoing the product

- Negotiating and closing the sale

- Post-sale transitional support or sales handoff

During presales, the sales engineer works alongside the account executive to discover the business need, build demos, and show them to prospects. The sales engineer is a technical role and creates demo applications. Sometimes you may hear the phrase "spinning up a new org." This simply means creating a new instance of the database to have a starting point. Demos are an important step in the software industry and information technology services industries. Since a lot of the work is customized, many customers have specific and unique requirements and like to see examples of the possibilities. Having sales engineers involved in the sales process can help the account executive understand what is realistic in a given time period and what the level of effort is for something that a client might ask for off the cuff.

Overall, the sales team helps the client make sure they are getting the right value for the solution presented. Oftentimes the licensing terms for buying software can be complex. The sales team advises on the different features to assist the clients in making the right decision. The solution engineer is often involved in responding to requests for proposals (RFPs) because they have knowledge of the technical details in RFP preparation. The client authors the RFP, and the sales team responds with a proposal. The presales group is also often closely aligned with marketing in producing marketing collateral and providing feedback on product roadmap items with product management groups.

Types of Contracts

Generally speaking, there are two types of contracts that are used to sell Salesforce delivery projects, fixed-price and time and materials (T&M).

Fixed price is riskier to the implementer or consulting firm because all the work needs to be done within the time and scope defined in the contract for the price agreed upon. This may seem like a way to make high profits by making sure the team is super-efficient and finishes everything early. On the other hand, if there are changes to the scope or the scope is not well defined, then the project takes longer to finish, and all the risk is on the project team.[1]

Managing risk on a fixed-cost project centers around scope management. One strategy is to include a sales engineer or other technical resource in the sales process. Sales engineers or delivery technical people should be involved in writing the contract for a fixed-price contract to make sure the scope is well defined. Hiring an experienced project manager who knows how to manage scope changes is also proven risk mitigation for this circumstance. It is important to set expectations in the beginning of any project, but on a fixed-price project it is important to communicate that that any changes in scope will require a discussion and a change order. Any request to change or add to the scope will need to be analyzed first to determine the impact to the timeline and resources and budget and communicated back to the client.

Every measurable factor of scope takes on heightened significance in a fixed-price contract. User stories with measurable acceptance criteria are important for testing, demos, and user acceptance testing to get to client sign-off.

A T&M contract is less risky to the implementer even if the scope is not well defined. Under this contract, the client agrees to pay based on time spent working. A budget ceiling is usually put in the contract, and the client pays up to that ceiling or maximum price or budget limit. The T&M contract dictates the terms under which the consulting team or individual on the team is staffed. For example, Pat is a data analyst consultant who gets staffed on the Widget Company project for 20 hours a week for a total of 180 hours for the entire project. This means that Pat is going to work on the project half time, since 40 hours a week is considered full time. She will most likely split her time between the Widget Company project and another project.

How to Get Staffed on a Project

After the sales team receives a signed contract back from the client, the consulting firm starts to pull together the team for the project. You might get hired by the consulting firm but not get immediately placed on a project. Usually, there are some temporary staffing decisions made before the final project team is complete. This is because there is no clear formula to predict when a contract will be signed or when everyone on both sides will be available to kick off the project. Some resources may already be staffed on projects that may be predicted to end at a certain date, but this can change if

---

[1] Lowden, G. & Thornton, J. (2015). The special challenges of project management under fixed-price contracts. Paper presented at PMI® Global Congress 2015—EMEA, London, England. Newtown Square, PA: Project Management Institute. https://www.pmi.org/learning/library/challenges-fixed-price-contracts-9640

there is a change order or other delay. So, the staffing plan starts out as an estimate of who will be on the project and when, and it is refined as factors become clearer.

On the Bench

If you are not currently on a project but are an employee of the consulting firm, then you are considered "on the bench," which is an idiom for players who are waiting to play a team sport but seated around the perimeter of the playing area and are waiting to play. Having a bench costs the consulting firm overhead, so consultants usually don't stay on it too long; however, if you find yourself on the bench, it is often a good time to help with business development or study for another Salesforce certification. It is common to be on the bench when you first start with a firm, when you are in between projects, or when you get kicked off a project, which unfortunately does happen to consultants from time to time.

It is also good to have an open mind with the projects that you are asked to join. Each project is a new experience and an opportunity for personal and professional growth. You really can't tell what a project is going to be like until you start it. Projects are what you make them. Your attitude makes a big difference. Big projects have challenges. Small projects have challenges. Some clients are easy to get along with. Some clients are not. Even if a client is nice and easy to get along with does not mean that they make decisions easily or understand Salesforce, which can be challenging. Learn more about client management in Chapter 13.

Centralized Staffing Model

A centralized staffing model is one where the consulting firm has a staffing department that helps plan and coordinate the resources for a project. The staffing group helps coordinate staffing for the consultant by working with account executives and delivery leaders to coordinate and plan into the future. There is a natural tension between the staffing department and the account leads who all want the best consultants for their projects. Their first pick may not be available when the projects are sold, because they are staffed or allocated for other projects. This tension is at the heart of what makes a delivery organization healthy. If you are good at your job, account executives and staffing may have a "tug of war" over where to place you. Both want you in the openings they have, and sometimes the negotiation goes on for a while. Oftentimes, account executives start planning which resources they prefer before the opportunity is even won. They do this to secure a consultant that they have confidence in.

The staffing manager might "pencil in" or tentatively plan the resource that they would like to have on a project. Sometimes, you might be staffed on a project, but then it falls through and you wind up on a totally different project. Sometimes this happens, because predicting the timing of a deal closing can be difficult. Sometimes the client delays signing the contract for one more round of review, and sometimes deals close very fast. It is perfectly normal to be penciled in on a project before the actual staffing plan is solidified. Expect changes while you wait for things to solidify, and don't take it personally.

Decentralized Staffing Model

Some companies do not have a staffing group, and it is up to the consultant to find their next project by working with their manager and networking within the firm. This happens in both big and small consulting firms. The decision to have a staffing department or role is a business decision. The service it provides is an operational cost, and some firms think there is value in having one, and some do not.

In a decentralized model, consultants tend to stay on projects for longer periods of time and integrate their activities with the client team more. If the consultant is the only person from the consulting firm on the project, this can feel a little like staff augmentation to the consultant, but reputable firms will be clear about the terms of the arrangement with the consultant. Consultants who work under a decentralized model may become nervous if their project ends, and they don't feel support from the firm to find a new project. Networking can be hard if you have spent all your time on your project and not interacting with consultants on other projects.

Having worked under both models, I think consultants are happier working in the centralized staffing model, because the staffing group works with consultant managers, and they both can advocate for the consultant. The staffing manager/consultant manager relationship creates a synergy that aids in uncovering career growth opportunities such as "stretch" roles that align with a consultant's goals and help in promotions. For example, if you have a goal of becoming a solution architect and have been on several projects as a business analyst, you might try a stretch role as a solution architect on your next project. Also, if you are a Salesforce consultant, you probably don't want to suddenly be moved to a project that is using a different technology because of all the time you have invested in learning Salesforce. The centralized staffing model mitigates this risk and also creates a mechanism that lets consultants move easier between projects and gain experience faster than staying on one project for two years.

How long you stay on a project is a personal preference. If you feel you are learning useful skills and adding value, then it doesn't matter if the project is long. On the other hand, you also learn useful skills and add value by being on multiple projects that change every three months. Many people don't like being on more than one project at a time because context switching can be difficult to maintain and lead to burnout.

Early in my career, I met a seasoned consultant who told me that he got antsy after about a year on a project. At the time I thought this sounded like a long time, but it is really not if you stay in consulting for a long time. No matter how long the project is, it is always good to take some time to regularly reflect on your goals. The world changes fast, and reassessing your goals is a gift to yourself. Check in with your mentor, manager, and the staffing department on a regular basis and have general conversations about how things are going. If you work remotely, ask them if they want to do a virtual coffee break, agree on a time, and send them a calendar invite.

Sales Handoff Meetings

The sales handoff is a meeting that takes place once a project is sold after the project is staffed. It is the time that the sales executive communicates pertinent information about the sale with the project team. This activity creates alignment between the sales and professional services groups. Professional services groups are also referred to as *delivery*. They are interchangeable terms in many organizations. A successful sales handoff creates aligned groups and makes the client experience better from the start. At its core, it is a communication exercise, and when it is skipped, it is obvious to the client and can be embarrassing for the delivery team; in short, it is not a good way for a project to begin.

Be sure to take some time to orient yourself around the big picture. What is the project about? What is the main use case or problem the team is trying to solve? Why are you on the project? If you can't answer these questions, then keep asking your project team until you get a sufficient answer. After you are on a project, you will be expected to know the answers to these questions sooner than you might expect, so be proactive from the start.

Sometimes sales handoffs occur before the whole team is fully onboarded onto the project. If you find yourself in this position, then ask if they recorded the meeting. It is a common practice to record sales handoffs for those who may join the project later. For example, sometimes certain roles such as quality assurance engineers or developers start projects after discovery (see Chapter 7 for more about discovery). If the sales handoff was not recorded, then during your onboarding or knowledge transfer meeting ask if there was a presentation or deck that the account executive can share with you. Sometimes consultants are thrown into projects with very little information. Other times too much detailed information is given. One caveat about sales handoff meetings to note is that in a bigger consulting firm, you may be far removed from the sales process and may never attend this type of meeting. Some projects are huge and have complicated contract vehicles, and the projects go on for years and years, especially if they are government projects. It is entirely possible that you could be brought into the middle of a project and read in during a knowledge transfer (KT) session with a member of the project team. This section covers consulting firms that have regular sales handoff meetings (or should).

The Sales Handoff Internal Meeting Presentation

The best sales handoffs are the ones where the account executive prepares a presentation beforehand and gives an overview of the company and summarizes major events of the sales cycle. Ideally, the account executive will come with a presentation that covers the following:

- The background of the company
- An overview of what was sold
- The timeline, scope, and budget
- Project assumptions and constraints
- Key client contact information, including titles and roles on the project
- Client idiosyncrasies
- Technologies

The Background of the Company

What does the company do? What industry does it serve? Is it a public or private company, or is it a nonprofit or government agency? If the company is public, then this tells you that there is public information available to read. Every year public companies are required to report filings called 10ks, which are annual reports to the Security and Exchange Commission (SEC). 10ks detail what the company does and include financial information. They are located on the SEC's website called EDGAR. If the company is a nonprofit, then the filing to check is the 990, which can be found on Guidestar. Company websites are the best source for private companies. But Dun and Bradstreet has limited information on company sales figures. If the project is for the government, then the government's website is the best source. Also, USA.gov has a directory of all the government departments and agencies. If you get staffed on a government project, it is important to know which of the 15 executive departments that your project sits under.

What Was Sold?

One of the worst outcomes at the beginning of a new project is when the delivery team is fuzzy on the details of the project and really doesn't know what the sales team has sold. When this happens, it becomes very easy to have client conversations where you sound like you don't know what is going on. This can become an embarrassing predicament and create a bad first impression in front of the client. It also makes it obvious that the consulting firm is not working together and the departments are not talking to each other. Needless to say, this is not a good way to kick off a project.

Specific questions to ask around what was sold on a Salesforce projects may include the following:

- What types of licenses were sold?
- How many users are there?
- How much data is there? Is a data migration needed?
- Is the work going to be done in a new org or an existing org?
- Was an integration sold?
  - How many integrations? What types? Is there any flexibility?
  - Does the client have access to their own data, or does an outside company manage access?
  - If they do not have access, who does, and will they give the client access within the timeline of the project?
  - Does the third-party company need to join the project, or will the client serve as the intermediary?
  - Is this a dependency on starting the project? (See Chapter 8 for more on dependencies.)

The Timeline, Scope, and Budget

The presentation should include a description of the length of the project, the amount, and the scope. This should also include a description of what is out of scope. Once the team knows what is out of scope, this information should be put in the risk log for monitoring throughout the life of the project. The presentation should also include a description of the roadmap or any future releases or plans that the account executive has made with the client. Other common questions include the following:

- Is there another company doing work on this project?

- Are we the primary contractor or the subcontractor?

- The answer to the previous question will tell you about the management structure of the project and who will be managing escalations and how many groups there are on the project.

The SOW

Above all else, make sure to read the statement of work (SOW) and know the answers to the relevant questions in this chapter. The SOW is the contract document that has the project information. Two common types were discussed earlier this chapter, fixed price and T&M. Ideally, the account executive will share the SOW beforehand, and the team can read through it and come to the meeting prepared with questions.

What Are the Assumptions?

Assumptions are very useful and clear up confusion right from the start. Undefined assumptions lead to misaligned expectations like in the tire swing example from Chapter 4. If assumptions are not defined up front, then projects can start to falter, and time gets wasted with unnecessary meetings where people don't communicate effectively. Writing out assumptions helps reduce project risk and issues.

An example of an assumption might be if the client would like a complex integration and need to procure a specific tool for the transformations, then this is a cost outside of the Salesforce license. The assumption would be that the client will buy the licenses needed for the tool to perform the integration. The client might assume that the migration can be done with Salesforce and they don't need to purchase anything else.

Another assumption could be that the delivery team will migrate their data, but it is up to the client to clean up "dirty data," meaning incomplete records and incorrect spellings of words in fields, for example. If a client does not know how to do this in an efficient way, then this would start a conversation around how they might approach this problem.

Client Idiosyncrasies

What should the team avoid saying? What shouldn't you say to the client? This comes up more times than you would think with seemingly innocent words. They are usually things that you can't predict and are situational. For example, I have been on three separate projects where the account executive advised us to avoid saying a specific word. There were words that only made sense in the context of those projects and were good to know ahead of time. The words? *Commercial, wiki,* and *Agile.*

What Is the Dynamic Between Business and IT?

It is also good to ask the account executive if they sold the project to the IT or business side of the company and what the relationship is like between the two groups. This is always an interesting dynamic and will tell you a lot about who is really in charge of the project. The business side makes the strategy for the company or organization. The IT group supports the business. Salesforce projects have the best chance at success when these two groups are aligned and supportive of one another.

Here is an example of what can happen if the two groups are not aligned. The account executive sells a Salesforce project to the CIO on the IT side of a company. The stakeholders on the business side might not understand what IT purchased. The business user might think that they are getting something different than what the CIO bought. And the reverse can be true, too. The business can buy the software and then hand it off to the IT team to work with the Salesforce implementation team. Successful Salesforce projects usually need input from both the IT and business sides.

Here are some common questions:

- Who bought the project? IT or business?
- What is their involvement and roles on the project?
- Who is in charge? Who is the decision-maker?
- Is there good communication between the two groups?

Introducing the Project Team to the Client

The account executive sometimes also holds an introductory call with the delivery team and the client. If the account executive doesn't do it, then it is set up by a relationship manager or project manager. Both meetings are important steps in the handoff between sales and delivery.

Technology

Sometimes a technology meeting is necessary between the project team and the client before the kickoff. This type of meeting saves time getting everyone on the project team set up in the client systems if the client technologies are going to be used in the project. For example, the client will also have to create Salesforce admin accounts for the project team and sometimes other work tracking and documentation systems such as Jira and/or SharePoint.

Summary

The two types of contracts typically seen in Salesforce delivery projects are fixed price and time and materials. Time and materials provides more scope flexibility and less risk to the project team. There are two types of staffing models that consulting firms use to place resources on projects. They are centralized and decentralized models. The sales handoff is an important time for consultants to gain an understanding of the sales cycle and important facts such as scope, budget, timeline, assumptions, expectations, client personality, and other client information. Have a standard list of questions ready to ask during the sales handoff. If the account executive doesn't answer them in the presentation, then make sure you ask.

Resources

Association of Record for Bid, Proposal, Business Development, Capture and Graphics. Professionals, `https://www.apmp.org/`

APMP Certification Program, `https://apmp.org/page/AccreditationProgram`

EDGAR, `https://www.sec.gov/edgar/searchedgar/companysearch.html`

Guidestar, `https://www.guidestar.org/search`

Dun and Bradstreet, `https://www.dnb.com/business-directory.html`

USA.gov, `https://www.usa.gov/federal-agencies`

Stages of a Project

Ramp-Up

In the beginning of a phase of a Salesforce project, there is a lot of preparation required to get the project off to a good start. Whether you are traveling to the client site for the first client meeting or working from home, there are travel resources that help you save time, increase efficiency, and reduce stress. If you are not traveling, then spending time on properly setting up your workspace setup is not something to skip. A proper workstation setup can help avoid potential injury.

Utilization, or the time you are expected to bill on a project, is an important metric to understand, especially if it is tied to a bonus or if there is a minimum that must be met.

You also must have a clear idea of the activities and deliverables that are associated with your role. This reduces team conflict and is an input to identifying people who can serve as your backup if needed.

Travel

So, you have been staffed on a project, have had the sales handoff meeting, and now the project manager is telling your team that kickoff will be "on-site." This means that the team will meet in person usually at the client offices. Time to travel!

© Heather Negley 2022
H. Negley, *The Salesforce Consultant's Guide*,
https://doi.org/10.1007/978-1-4842-7960-1_7

How Much Will I Travel?

A lot of new consultants ask about travel when they are interviewing. Recruiters often want to know how much travel someone is willing to do. It is a question that comes up often. In my experience, I have found that if the consulting firm wants you to commit to 80 percent travel, this usually means traveling every week, Monday through Thursday, and then working from home on Fridays.

The norm is for clients to pick up the travel expenses for the consultant. In fact, sometimes projects require that the consultants work from the client's office location. When this is the case, consultants will probably work on-site Monday through Thursday and then travel home on Thursday evening so they can work from home on Friday. In other circumstances, the client may not have a big budget for travel, so consultants may travel only for important events in the project such as kickoff and discovery and do the rest of the project remotely. Some consulting companies have a workforce that is completely remote, so teams work remotely even within their own organizations. They use teleconferences such as Webex, Zoom, or Google Meet and instant messaging technologies such as Slack, Microsoft Teams, or Google Hangouts.

If the consulting firm requires a 25 percent commitment to travel, then the expectations are that you will be traveling on-site for important meetings such as kickoff and discovery and the rest of the work will be done remotely or at the local consulting office. The amount of travel required really depends. In some firms, consultants have to be willing to travel 80 percent of the time as a prerequisite to getting hired. However, since most of the world had to suddenly start working remotely during the COVID-19 pandemic that started in 2020, there are more and more remote work arrangements than ever before.

If you are planning on traveling for your project, knowing how to balance time is an important strategy to minimize stress. Schedule your transportation via Lyft or Uber the night before to make sure that there is someone available to drive you to the airport or train station. Build in time for travel delays. For example, if the kickoff meeting is the first thing in the morning, then it may make sense to travel the night before. That way, if there are any travel delays, you will not have to worry about being late for the morning meeting. If the kickoff meeting is in the afternoon and your flight is short, figure out if there is enough time to travel first thing in the morning and still build in time for potential delays.

Leave yourself ample time to arrive. Some teams coordinate travel logistics and meet each other at the airport together to save on rental car costs. The MileIQ app logs miles and can be helpful if you are renting a car and need to keep track of miles driven. Make sure you know the address of the location where the kickoff is located beforehand and how long it takes to get there from the airport. Meet up with your team before kickoff for last-minute preparation at the hotel or for breakfast/lunch near the client location before kickoff and then walk in together.

Airport Hacks

Traveling can be stressful, but if you are well organized and manage your time efficiently, it also can be a fun time to meet and connect with people in person and strengthen relationships. There are many airport shortcuts to save time and minimize stress. From faster check-ins to airport clubs, there are several ways to make the flight enjoyable. Here are a few tips to save you time and manage stress at the airport.

CLEAR. This program uses biometrics such as your irises or fingerprints to prove your identity instead of traditional methods like your passport or driver's license. If you have signed up for the CLEAR service beforehand, then the only thing you have to show to prove your identity at the airport is your fingerprints or the irises of your eyes. The CLEAR system uses your unique biometric information and turns it into an encrypted code that is distinctive to you. When you go to the airport, you have your fingers or eyes scanned by the CLEAR technology. There should be a CLEAR lane at TSA check-in points. Then go on to the security check.

TSA PreCheck. This is a program run by the Transportation Security Administration (TSA) and is another time-saving program that you have to register for beforehand. It is a way to bypass the long security lines by going through a background check and paying a fee beforehand. If you have TSA PreCheck, then you don't have to take off your shoes, belts, or light jackets when going through security. It makes the process faster and cuts down on long wait times. It takes a few weeks to get approved, so you should plan this ahead of time.

Also, TSA has a list of their top travel tips on its website. Since rules change from time to time, it is good to check this list before your flight. Some of the more common rules are the liquid rule, which limits liquids to travel-sized containers that are 3.4 ounces (100 milliliters) or less per item. TSA also has an extensive list of items that you are allowed to bring, which can be handy if you are wondering about a particular item. It is a pretty long list and has items from blankets and bread to flowers and hair dryers. All are okay to bring. If you have to go through the security line, then wear shoes that are easy to take on and off such as slip-on shoes and socks so you don't have to walk barefoot on the airport floor.

Airline Clubs. Airline clubs are special areas set aside for travelers to eat and relax. They have features such as food and drink, business centers, fast WiFi connections, showers, and lounges. You can either join an airline club through the airline directly to get access to their airport lounge or use Lounge Buddy to search for a club by city or airport and book by the hour through their website.

Mileage Programs. Join the mileage program for the airline to accumulate points that can later be used for free travel and upgrades. Hotels such as Marriott or Hilton also have similar programs that can save money for frequent travelers.

Items for the plane. Bring your own blanket and noise canceling headphones and a backup power supply. Download Netflix or Hulu ahead of time to watch movies. Buy a bottle of water once you get through security for the flight to prevent dehydration or, better yet, bring an empty water bottle and fill it up at a water bottle filling station at the gate.

Once you land, FLIO is a useful app to use if you are in an airport that is unfamiliar to you. This free app will tell you where the ground transportation is located and any other useful tips to know about the airport. For example, sometimes there are designated areas for Uber and Lyft rides (*rideshares*) that aren't immediately apparent because they are often located at a different location than the taxis. FLIO will explain the distinction that a particular airport makes around this.

Travel Reimbursement

If you don't have access to the corporate credit card, then then you will probably pay out of pocket and get reimbursed. The client usually pays for the travel, but it has to be written in the contract, and every contract is different, so make sure to talk to your project manager about the specific constraints around hotel costs and meals.

Usually, the consultant pays for the trip and then submits an expense report at the end of the trip. Save those receipts. Better yet, take a picture of them right when you make the purchase. It is easy to lose receipts when you are in a rush, and the best consultants I know take a picture of their receipt right when they pay for something. Uber emails you your receipt, which is very convenient. There are several free receipt apps. Expensify is often recommended by journalists who write top ten lists on this topic. The service costs $5 per month or is free with a limit of 10 receipts per month.

Sometimes the project has a per diem, which is a set maximum amount for food, lodging, and incidentals that a client will reimburse a consultant without having to produce a receipt. Make sure you talk to your project manager and you are clear on the travel reimbursement arrangements because these arrangements can and often do change from project to project.

Working from Home

More and more people are working remotely. This provides a lot of flexibility for a better work-life balance. But it is still important to set up a healthy, ergonomic workspace at home.

First, make sure you have a comfortable place to work but not too comfortable, like not the couch. Some days it may seem like a more comfortable option to work from your couch or bed because you are tired, but it's really not a good idea. Please don't work from your bed. Along with the ergonomic problems, it sets up a whole lot of other potential issues like not paying attention, falling asleep, or getting the conferencing software settings wrong and inadvertently turning your camera on, allowing people to see you lying in your bed. Unfortunately, I've seen this happen, and it's embarrassing for everyone.

Once you work from home for a while, it can be easy to forget the correct angles for your arms and eyes to the keyboard and monitor. Take a look at Figure 7-1 and make sure that the angles line up correctly. Is your keyboard low enough, or are you reaching up too far? Is your neck bent down? When you don't have an ergonomic setup, most people end up sitting rounded over. Don't hunch over your desk. This is called *text neck*. It is when you bend your chin down to look at your phone or computer. This seemingly small movement puts a great deal of weight on your neck and upper back muscles. Over time it can lead to health problems. Offices usually spend a great deal of time and effort to make workstations ergonomic for their workers. This may not have been something that you have considered for your home office. But it is worth thinking through and asking your employer for help with the correct setup.

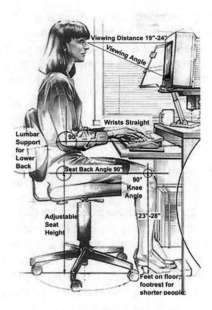

Figure 7-1. Example of ergonomic body angles while seated at a desk (Source: Wikimedia Commons)

Also, a lot of people get standing desks so they aren't sitting all the time. But, even with standing desks, you have to make sure that the angles are right so that you are not putting too much pressure on your neck. The key is to make sure to move around often. Walk around. Don't stand or sit in one position for too long. Changing position frequently gives one area of your body a break while another takes over for a while. Pomodoro timers are good to use to remind yourself to take short breaks.

Setting up two monitors also makes working easier. A laptop along with a second monitor will allow you to glance back and forth between screens. This makes working easier, because it cuts down on the opening and closing of browser windows. If you have two monitors, look into the monitor with the camera during a conference call. Put the meeting window on the monitor with the camera so it doesn't look like you are looking away from people when you speak.

Make sure your workstation is well lit. Place a light on your desk and have it illuminate your screen. Don't place it behind you, or it will make you look like a silhouette. Figure 7-2 is an example of a light source coming from behind people. The light is the furthest thing from the camera. It casts a dark outline on the people. This is not what you want. In Figure 7-3, the light is on the women's faces. The source of the light is behind the camera, and it is lighting the faces of the women.

Figure 7-2. Example of a silhouette. The light source is in front of the camera

Figure 7-3. Example of lighting coming from behind the camera

Take some time to assess what is behind you. Is it tidy, and is not unnecessarily distracting? That's your goal. You don't have to sit in front of a completely white wall; just make sure your background is uncluttered and calm so the focus is on you.

Another option is to use the background feature in a conference application such as Zoom to project a background image behind you. This completely blocks out everything behind you. For example, you can pick a picture of the Golden Gate Bridge in San Francisco as your background. I was recently on a project team where everyone on the team used these backgrounds, so I decided to try it. I had tried this feature before but wasn't a fan because I found that the edges of my head seemed cut off. I mentioned this to my teammates who told me that simply placing green posterboard behind you will stop this effect. As you may already know, this is called a *green screen* and is used in film production and is basically used to drop things into the background. It doesn't have to be green, but green is often used because it doesn't conflict with skin color. If you use Zoom, there is a setting to turn on that will create the right effect, but you need the actual green screen behind you for it to work. And it really can be as simple as buying a piece of cardboard like the one in Figure 7-4 from a craft store. I have also listed a link to a portable one from Amazon that attaches to the back of your chair in the "Resources" section at the end of this chapter.

Figure 7-4. A do-it-yourself green screen can be made with green cardboard found at a craft store

If your meeting is remote, then unmute yourself and turn on your camera video when introducing yourself. Then mute your audio again so background noise does not distract the other people on the call. It might sound obvious, but people like to see other people, so it is more engaging and will help you build a better interpersonal connection if you turn on your camera. If you have to leave during a call but don't want to interrupt the speaker, then write a note in the chat that says "be right back," and when you return, write "back" so that everyone knows you have returned. Also, if you have to leave a call early or one that is running over, then write a note in the chat before you drop so that the participants know you have left the call. You can simply write, "I have to drop for another call" or "I have a hard stop and have to drop. Thanks."

Utilization

Once you get staffed on a project, you may start tracking your utilization, especially if the firm you are working for has utilization goals. Utilization is a measure of the amount of work that you contribute to the consulting firm. Consulting firms use this to measure your value to the firm or, in other words, how much money you are making them. It is calculated by your billable hours projects divided by the number of working hours in a week, which is usually 40 hours. So if you work 40 billable hours in a week, your utilization is 100 percent. If you work less than 40 hours in the week, then your utilization goes down. If you work overtime, then your utilization goes up and can go over 100 percent.

The utilization calculation is spread across the year and excludes holidays and vacations. If you work at a place with unlimited PTO and the firm gives out utilization bonuses based on targets, then you will want to make sure that you ask the total number of billable hours the firm is using for the year and plan accordingly. Some consulting firms have targets or a minimum utilization percentage that you have to reach in order to get a bonus at the end of the year. Other firms pay higher bonuses for exceeding targets such as working more than 40 hours a week. Every firm is different. Keep in mind that time spent on the bench will lower your utilization since you are not doing billable work. Conversely, some firms do not have utilization targets or bonuses at all.

A common question that consultants debate often is if it is ethical to bill a client for time that you are not in front of your computer but thinking about solutions to help them solve their problems. One way to think through this conundrum is to ask yourself if you were hired to think. A lot of IT work is problem solving. If you take a walk and your mind is still working on solving the problem and helps you make progress toward solving it, then I would consider that billable work. If, on the other hand, you are driving your kids around and thinking about all the things on your to-do list, some of which include tasks you need to get completed for work, then I would not consider this billable work. But there are nuances to this, and it can be endlessly debated.

Know Your Role

Your project team will come together soon after the sales handoff to talk about the project plan. The project manager or lead will schedule this first team meeting. It is common for a new team to experience natural disorganization and confusion when it comes together for the first time.[1] To help mitigate this risk, the project manager will preemptively create organized structures for easy communication and documentation such as team rosters, agendas, communication plans, access to work ticketing and instant messaging tools, as well as other plans to help the team assimilate and mitigate uncertainties and inefficiencies.

One important task to set up a project team for success is to communicate the roles assigned. These are usually listed in the statement of work. Even more important is for each person on the team to know from the start which person is filling each particular role. Most importantly, and I cannot stress this enough, it is important that every team member knows which activities are assigned to which roles. If you do not know who is responsible for a specific

---

[1] RACI, Paladino, Darren, Project Management Institute, Retrieved 5/15/2021, https://www.projectmanagement.com/contentPages/wiki.cfm?ID=234008&thisPageURL=/wikis/234008/RACI#1

activity, it is important to ask. You may have identified a gap that was overlooked and needs discussion. Don't assume that someone else knows and wait. Proactive action in consulting makes life easier in the long run.

Some project managers create clarity in this area by creating activity charts. A team can split up activities in many ways. The best teams set clear responsibilities but also talk about who can back up another team member if they are in a pinch. This gives teams flexibility.

For example, in this use case, Main Street Bank is setting up a Financial Services Cloud org. An *org* is a term used in the Salesforce ecosystem. It simply means an instance of the platform that you can log in to. Main Street Bank bought Financial Services Cloud licenses. When a user logs into an org, they can see the preconfigured set of objects and relationships associated with the licenses that they purchased. The objects are represented as horizontal tabs across the top of the screen. This gives them access to make applications tailored to their use case. The distinctions in the types of licenses are outside the scope of this book. But the general common knowledge is that Salesforce has many types of license types. Many end with the name *cloud*. Examples include Sales Cloud, Service Cloud, Marketing Cloud, Experience Cloud, etc., and others have unique names such Knowledge, Shield, or CPQ. The licenses can be mixed and matched depending on the type of functionality needed. Then users have access to a specific configuration of objects and relationships and/ or functionality for common use cases in particular industries.

So, in this example, Main Street Bank bought the Financial Services Cloud licenses because it wants to connect or integrate their customer bank account information into Salesforce. An integration allows data to be passed from one database to another database. This is an overly simplified definition. In fact, there are a lot of rules and specifications that go into this. If you are interested in learning more about Salesforce integrations, then I highly recommend reading David Masri's *Developing Data Migrations and Integrations with Salesforce*.

As the team gets organized to start working on the project, the project manager may make a chart similar to the one in Figure 7-5, which lists all the major activities and the role that is responsible for performing the work. The chart also lists the name of the person who is assigned to the role. By assigning activities to roles, it becomes seamless for a person filling a role to read all the activities for which the role is responsible.

Activity	Role	Name
Take Meeting notes	Business Analyst	James Anderson
Create Project Plan	Project Manager	Emily Clarke
Schedule and Run Meetings	Project Manager	Emily Clarke
Create Kick-off Deck	Project Manager	Emily Clarke
Create Meeting Agendas	Project Manager	Emily Clarke
Compile Client Project Team info and Share with team	Project Manager	Project Manager
Send project Status Reports to Client	Project Manager	Emily Clarke
Create Backlog	Business Analyst	James Anderson
Write User Stories	Business Analyst	James Anderson
Create Epics	Solution Architect	Gina Garcia
Create Data Transformations	Data Architect	Layla Rafftery
Perform Mappings	Business Analyst, Data Architect, Product Owner	James Anderson, Layla Rafftery, Owen Wilson
Migrate Data	Data Architect	Layla Rafftery
Prioritize Stories	Product Owner	Owen Wilson
Create Solution	Solution Architect	Gina Garcia
Give Demo	Business Analyst	James Anderson
Write Test Scripts	Business Analyst	James Anderson
Write Training Plan	Project Manager	Emily Clarke
Perform Configurations	Solution Architect, Business Analyst	Gina Garcia, James Anderson
Write Apex Trigger	Developer	Amanda Kim
Perform Train-the-Trainer	Solution Architect	Gina Garcia
Write Release Plan	Solution Architect	Gina Garcia
Deploy code	Data Architect, Solution Architect, Developer	Layla Rafftery, Gina Garcia, Amanda Kim

Figure 7-5. Major activities and the roles responsible for the work

Activities assigned to roles can change and often do change from project to project. You may even have more than one role on a project. This project has five project team members: a project manager, business analyst, data architect, solution architect, and developer. In this example, notice how the business analyst is the role who writes the test scripts. This is because there is no dedicated quality assurance engineer on the project. On smaller projects, the budget is not large enough to hire all the roles in a theoretically ideal scenario. In reality, members of the team will have to become skilled in many areas, not just the ones that they may consider their specialty. This makes them well-rounded and high-value consultants in the long run. Even if you do projects with the same general use case, teams are always different, as unique as people and their skills. You can do the same role from project to project as a consultant, but that doesn't mean you will necessarily do the same activities each time.

Figure 7-6 has an activity list for the same use case with different roles assigned to the project. The activities are the same, but they are assigned to different roles. This project team is smaller with only four project team members: a solution architect, business analyst, technical architect, and quality assurance engineer. In this project, the quality assurance engineer writes the test scripts as one would expect instead of the business analysts like in the previous example. But note how the technical architect migrates the data since there is not a dedicated data architect role as in the previous example.

Activity	Role	Name
Take Meeting notes	Business Analyst	James Anderson
Create Project Plan	Solution Architect	Emily Clarke
Schedule and Run Meetings	Solution Architect	Emily Clarke
Create Kick-off Deck	Solution Architect	Emily Clarke
Create Meeting Agendas	Business Analyst	James Anderson
Compile Client Project Team info and Share with team	Business Analyst	James Anderson
Send project Status Reports to Client	Solution Architect	Emily Clarke
Create Backlog	Business Analyst	James Anderson
Write User Stories	Business Analyst	James Anderson
Create Epics	Solution Architect	Emily Clarke
Create Data Transformations	Technical Architect	Layla Rafftery
Perform Mappings	Business Analyst, Technical Architect, Product Owner	James Anderson, Layla Rafftery, Owen Wilson
Migrate Data	Technical Architect	Layla Rafftery
Create Solution	Solution Architect	Emily Clarke
Give Demo	Business Analyst	James Anderson
Write Test Scripts	Quality Assurance Engineer	Amanda Kim
Perform Configurations	Solution Architect, Business Analyst	Emily Clarke, James Anderson
Deployment	Technical Architect	Layla Rafftery

Figure 7-6. Major activities assigned to different roles responsible for the work

Sometimes projects need a more detailed level of expectation setting and alignment with the client, especially if the team is part of a larger team with different workstreams running in parallel. For example, there could be a separate data team running their own sprints in parallel to a development team. Whatever the scenario, the project manager will make a determination if more clarity is needed for the team, and if so, they may create an advanced chart of project responsibilities called a RACI chart. RACI stands for Responsible, Accountable, Consulted, and Informed and can be a useful tool if the team needs detailed clarity on not only who is responsible for doing the work as in the previous two examples but also who is ultimately responsible for task and who just needs to be consulted perhaps for validating a solution and who just needs to be kept informed. See Figure 7-7 for an example of a RACI chart for this project.

Activity	Business Analyst	Solution Architect	Technical Architect	Product owner	Quality Assurance Engineer
Take Meeting notes	RA	CI	CI	CI	CI
Create Project Plan	CI	RA	CI	CI	CI
Schedule and Run Meetings	CI	RA	I	I	I
Create Kick-off Deck	CI	RA	CI	I	I
Create Meeting Agendas	R	ACI	I	I	I
Compile Client Project Team info and Share with team	RCI	ACI	CI	CI	CI
Send project Status Reports to Client	CI	RA	CI	I	CI
Create Backlog	R	A	CI	CI	I
Write User Stories	R	A	I	CI	I
Create Epics	CI	RA	CI	I	I
Create Data Transformations	CI	CI	RA	CI	I
Perform Mappings	RA	RA	RA	RACI	I
Migrate Data	CI	CI	RA	I	I
Create Solution	CI	RA	CI	CI	I
Give Demo	RA	CI	CI	CI	CI
Write Test Scripts	CI	I	I	I	RA
Perform Configurations	RA	R	CI	I	I
Deployment	CI	CI	RA	CI	I

Figure 7-7. RACI chart

Summary

The amount of travel that is required by the consultant depends on the project and what the client wants. Be sure to ask specific questions on travel requirements before you start a project. There are more and more remote Salesforce projects than ever before. If you work from home, take some time to set up an ergonomic workstation to avoid injury and take breaks that involve moving away from your computer.

No matter, your work location, the number of hours that you are allocated to a project can affect your utilization score and bonus, so keep an eye on this and make sure the goals set by management are realistic.

Finally, know your role and the activities associated with it, and make sure your teammates know theirs as well.

Resources

Ground transportation apps, available either from Google Play for a phone with the Android operating system or from the App Store for an iPhone

> Lyft, a modern day taxi that matches riders with divers using an on demand service model, `https://www.lyft.com/`
>
> Uber, competitor to Lyft, `https://www.uber.com/`
>
> MileIQ app, logs rental car miles, `https://www.mileiq.com/`

CLEAR registration, `https://www.clearme.com/`

TSA, top travel tips, `https://www.tsa.gov/travel/travel-tips`

TSA, What Can I Bring, `https://www.tsa.gov/travel/security-screening/whatcanibring/all`

Lounge Buddy, `https://www.loungebuddy.com/`

FLIO, free directories and layout maps for airports, `https://www.flio.com/`

Expensify, receipt tracking, `https://bit.ly/3BXeMia`

Portable Yacikos BackUp Power Supply, for a smartphone `https://amzn.to/2V3mnLH`

Tomato Timer, used for taking short breaks using the Pomodoro Technique `https://tomato-timer.com/`

Kickoff and Discovery

The kickoff meeting is one of the most important meetings on a project. It is the time that the team makes the all-important first impression and talks to the client about their goals for the project. The project methodology is also taught to the client.

During discovery the project team conducts business analysis using a variety of techniques to gain an understanding of the current and future processes. Project members write users stories to prepare for the build phase.

Also during this stage of a project, the team will start to go through the stages of team cohesion which include forming, storming, norming, performing, and adjourning.

What Is Kickoff?

Kickoff marks the official, formal start of a project and is the first meeting in a series of discovery meetings at the beginning of a project. Kickoff and discovery are usually a combined event with meetings spread over several days. This first meeting in the series, called the *kickoff meeting*, is a meeting where the client and the delivery team meet to "kick off" the project. This term is derived football where the player kicks the ball at the beginning of the

© Heather Negley 2022
H. Negley, *The Salesforce Consultant's Guide*,
https://doi.org/10.1007/978-1-4842-7960-1_8

game. Kickoffs are usually held in person at the client's office, but they can also be held remotely for smaller projects, when the client does not have the budget or see the need to pay for the consultants to travel to their offices, or when there is a pandemic.

During kickoff and discovery, you will learn about the client's business needs. It is a time where you get to know the client and start to establish a relationship ideally as a long-term trusted adviser. The client has to give up some control in order to give you their trust. Like any relationship, this will take time, but this is a great time to start establishing your credibility. If you go in with the intention to deliver a solution and/or advice in line with the client's best interest and you communicate this from the start, then you are off to a good start toward building trust. Over time, your advice will become more and more valued.

Executive sponsorship is vital to project success, so their attendance at these meetings is important. These are often the people with decision-making authority on the project. Sometimes they are the people who sign the SOWs. Schedule regular meetings with sponsors throughout the project as well to keep them informed and to raise important issues.

Kickoffs are also a good time to confirm everything that you heard in the sales handoff meeting to make sure you are aligned. Don't be surprised if expectations need to be reset. Make sure to go over the goals of the project and the measures of success.

Interpersonal Tips

There are some basic interpersonal do's and don'ts to remember during client kickoffs. A commonsense one is to dress appropriately. If you are traveling in person, then ask about the dress code of the client office ahead of time and then try to dress a little nicer.

Less intuitive tips include not getting too familiar too fast, which means don't get too personal with clients too quickly. You might be friendly, but be careful of sharing too much information about yourself right off the bat during. Don't be in a rush. Relationships take time to build and usually start out with a lot of listening, which helps you tune into the personality of the other person. Understanding how to read the social cues of other people goes a long way toward developing emotional intelligence and can save you from a lot of uncomfortable situations.

You want to become a trusted adviser, but kickoff might not be the best time to tell everyone about your funniest and most embarrassing moment in life. Sometimes there is an ice-breaker exercise where everyone shares something interesting about themselves. Read the room and consider the audience if this comes up. If your client is a toy company, then sharing your favorite toy as a kid may be appropriate, especially if that company made it, but if your client is more serious, then sharing something less personal might be better for a first introduction.

Another tip is to refrain from introducing yourself to your teammates in front of the client. This diminishes the appearance of strong team cohesion and gives the client the impression that the team is weak because the team members don't know each other. This is a legitimate concern on its own, but the nature of the work and methodology requires the team to get to know each other quickly, and each member is chosen for their skills. In fact, most teams go through the team cohesion process of forming, storming, norming, and performing, which I explain in more detail later in this chapter under "Team Cohesion." These introductions happen more times than you might think, so it is something to be aware of. If you get caught off-guard, then you can say "Nice to see you again" or "Nice to see you in person." More often than not, you will have had some type of interaction with your teammates before kickoff.

If the project is in another country, then research the business etiquette and cultural norms in that country to avoid any blunders or unintended slights. See Chapter 10 for more on communicating in different cultural contexts.

Understand Client Vision and Use Cases

The client's vision for a project is the overarching picture that they are trying to achieve. It is often tied to their strategic plan and has measurable goals. For example, a Salesforce consultant usually works on digital modernization goals.

A use case is a scenario that defines the way that a user wants to interact or "use" a software system. Use cases are often written out as user stories with acceptance criteria. (See "Writing User Stories" later in this chapter.)

By kickoff, you should be familiar with the use case from the sales handoff, from reading the SOW, and from general discussion and knowledge transfer with your team. Kickoff and discovery is a time to listen to the client talk about their vision and use cases from their point of view in full detail. Usually the consulting team prepares a presentation for the kickoff meeting that includes high-level information such as team member names, timeline, roles, and the purpose of the project, as well as the client vision, goals, and success metrics. Success metrics are measurable outcomes and can also be referred to as key performance indicators (KPIs). Salesforce is a tool that can be used to help reach these goals. It is important to remember and remind the client if necessary that Salesforce is a tool and not a strategy. It is a configurable platform that can help you reach and measure goals.

For example, Main Street Bank has a digital modernization vision with the goal to allow users to see aggregated data from all their bank branches in real time. Some of their measurable goals may include the following:

- What is the total value of deposits from all branches?
- How many accounts have been opened today, and who opened them?
- What is the total number of accounts?

The solution architect will design a solution that will have the answer to these questions built into the system and accessible via reports or dashboards.

Project Methodology

Kickoff and discovery should have a project methodology session. This session is an overview of how the client and project teams will come together to work on the project. Every firm has its own unique method for delivering projects. A lot of firms use a combination of Waterfall and Agile methodologies. They gather all the requirements up front like in Waterfall and may help the client with prioritizing the user stories. Others write the business requirements but ask the client to write the acceptance criteria, which is the second half of a user story.

Sometimes consulting firms name their methodologies, so the session title may reflect this and may say, Connor's Consulting Semi-Agile Methodology, The Ella Way: Agile 101, or something similar. These types of sessions, usually led by the project manager or team lead, are intended to inform the client team about how the project will be structured day by day. There is a lot of uncertainty in the beginning of a project, and these sessions help set expectations with the client ahead of time. Business stakeholders usually do not spend their day to day working on IT delivery projects and may not understand the time commitment that is expected from them. Also, they may not understand the types of meetings that the Salesforce project team needs to have with them.

In the next few chapters, I will walk you through the parts of a semi-agile methodology project, from gathering requirements to business analysis and writing user stories and process flows in discovery to setting up an Agile backlog. These are all fundamental steps in the lifecycle of a Salesforce project. I am going to explain concepts in Scrum, which is a popular Agile-specific methodology. In Chapter 9, I will explain the ceremonies during the development process, and in Chapter 10, I explain user acceptance testing and deploying the app. All these sections are part of a delivery methodology and something that should be presented and explained to a client during kickoff.

What Is Discovery?

Discovery is a phase at the beginning of the project. The goal of discovery meetings is to understand the client's current business processes and procedures. Discovery is usually combined with the kickoff meeting and is the beginning phase in a project where information is gathered from the client through interviews, discussions, documentation, and demonstrations of existing technology. As a Salesforce consultant participating in discovery, it is important to be curious. You are there to discover.

There are usually a series of discovery meetings on data or technologies depending on the scope of the project with a full agenda spanning several days or weeks with a variety of the activities and meetings specific to that project. But at a high level, the team learns definitions of business terms important to the business as well as processes, roles, data, and procedures.

In some circumstances, the consulting firm may sell the discovery phase of a project as a stand-alone project. This is sometimes done if the scope is large, and it may take a few months to gather all the information needed. The deliverable or work product for this type of project is a plan forward, such as a roadmap that may detail releases out in years. Roadmap projects are projects to plan releases across projects. How to build a roadmap is outside the scope of this book, but if you are interested in more details, then see "How to Build a Roadmap" in "Resources" at the end of this chapter. There also may be a deliverable of a solution design plan, which lays out the technical design plan around the data model and processes.

For a small, traditional delivery project, a common cadence is for a team to spend two weeks gathering requirements during the discovery phase and then have three two-week sprints, followed by a month of training, UAT, and deployment. (See Figure 8-1.)

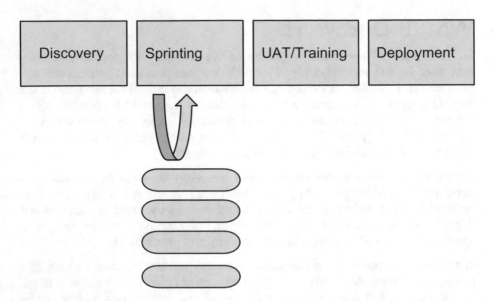

Figure 8-1. A common cadence is for a team to spend two weeks gathering requirements during the discovery phase and then three two-week sprints, followed by a month of training, UAT, and deployment

Different roles may lead the discovery session depending on the content. Usually the business analyst leads it to figure out the existing and future processes, but sometimes the solution architect leads discovery depending on the makeup of the team. Sometimes the technical architect will lead a technology session to discuss the technologies in the company and the architecture plan. The project manager may keep the team on track if one person goes into a lengthy detailed explanation that causes information overload. While discussing details, it is important to monitor the group for tangents and "rabbit holes" with excessive details that can throw the team off-course and waste valuable time. Sometimes it makes more sense to schedule follow-up meetings to "dive deeper" into specific topics. Other times, higher-level decisions are made, and the deep-dive meetings are not needed at all because they are no longer relevant.

Validate who the note-taker is before each session begins. All notes should have a section for action items, which is anything that needs to be followed up on later. Record the meetings if you think they may be helpful in the future. You may not want to go back and listen to three days of recordings, so try to create important recordings and not add to the amount of information to review if it is not needed.

Business Analysis

Business analysis is the process of observing, documenting, planning and analyzing the processes and business rules in a company. During discovery, a business analyst will utilize several methods to collect this information. To be good at this skill, you should be curious, observative, and analytical. If you approach discovery as a challenge that will have a positive outcome, then you will be guided by optimism, which is an important component of resilience and will help you keep pushing forward in spite of difficulties. See Chapter 11 for more on resilience.

Current State and Future State

There are many methods available to capture business processes. One common technique is to document the current business process or "current state" in order to understand the baseline or starting point from which changes to a system will be made. This is done by interviewing key stakeholders and asking them to explain their current challenges. Other techniques include asking stakeholders to conduct demonstrations of the current system and to have round-table discussions and using a white board to capture key points. During this type of session, it is a good time to ask the client what they do and do not like about the current process and system. This is important information and key to building a useful solution. Not only does it help bring clarity to the current state, but it will also help to start to shape a future state.

The business analyst will make a decision to focus on one process, system, or type of user also called a *persona*. For example, a customer service rep may give a demo of their current database and give a walk-through of their current help-desk process. The customer service rep is a persona in this example. Projects may have one persona or many personas. The more personas in a process, the more complicated the processes are because each persona goes through the process with rules assigned to their individual persona. One common example of this is the ability to create, read, edit, or delete (CRED) data. These rules may be different for each persona. Learn more about CRED in Chapter 9.

Some clients will have tons of documentation and may have even written up their own requirements, while others won't have one single thing. For example, I once spent the summer on a project in a business analyst role where my sole task was to help the client review and rewrite 300 user stories that had been rewritten 3 times in previous years. It took the whole summer because there was a committee of people wordsmithing the requirements. That was the project where I learned that using the word "select" was a better word choice in a requirement than "click" because "click" assumes a mouse click while "select" does not. The intention was to try not to include design in the requirement, and a mouse click was considered design.

You may find that the stakeholders are from many different departments and do not work with each other too often and have never sat down in a room together to discuss their processes. Departments may have their own disparate siloed processes and databases and data that is not easily shared between departments. Maybe one department emails a report to another department on a regular basis because they do not share a database. There may be good reasons for this, or it may be something that just grew organically without a bigger plan to include other departments. As a Salesforce consultant, it is your job to ask these questions and to dig into the reasons why the current state is set up the way it is. You have to be ready for anything. Conversely, you may discover that the team you are working with is a high-performance team and very technical and you are there to help them create something cutting-edge and highly automated. Your job will be to teach them the Crawl, Walk, Run approach and advise them on the pros and cons that come with a high level of automation.

Process Flows

Business analysts often document their work using the Unified Modeling Language (UML), which is a standard notation for modeling software diagrams. Popular tools used to model diagrams include Visio, Lucid Charts, diagrams.net/draw.io, and others. One of the models seen often in Salesforce projects is called the *process flow*. The process flow documents a business process in detail. It can include swim lanes for the persona, squares for the process step, and diamonds for decision points. Figure 8-2 shows a simple customer service process with two personas, the customer, and the customer service representative. It details the process that starts with the following:

1. A customer submits an email request.

2. The customer service representative reviews the application/request and decides if the application meets the criteria needed.

3. If the application is not complete and does not meet the proper criteria, the process begins again with the customer having to correct the information and submit another email request. The details of how "criteria" is defined is on the data level and is not documented in a process flow. Instead, it is written in the user story.

4. If the application does meet the criteria needed, the customer service representative sends an email to the customer and changes the status of the case. Of course, most processes are more complicated than this one, but this example has some of the most basic elements.

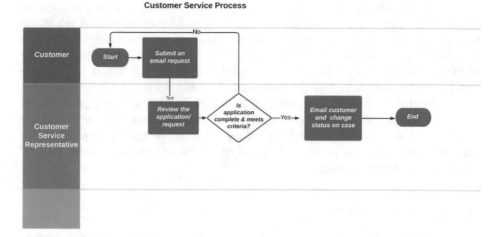

Figure 8-2. Customer service process

Writing User Stories

In a project operating under the Waterfall methodology, requirements are written during discovery. Requirements list the functionality that the system should have. This is not the preferred method on an Agile project, where user stories are written instead of requirements. User stories are behavior-based, written from the point of view of archetypes such as a role in a company, or persona. They have two parts, the scenario and the acceptance criteria. A user story is written from the perspective of the person performing the process and in a style that separates behavior from the tool, technology, or solution. This is so the best solution can be chosen after the story is written. For example, even using the word "click" instead of "select" may imply a solution because it is possible to pick an option without clicking with a mouse. In addition, Waterfall requirements are not behavior based. They are a list of functional aspects of a system.

A common syntax for a user story is as follows: "As a" (person), "I want" (to do something) "so that" (the reason). Here is an example of a user story written from the point of view of a customer service agent:

> As a customer service representative, I want to record a customer interaction so that I can see it keep track of the issue until it is resolved.

In this example, the persona of a customer service representative is describing a business process of saving information from a customer and tracking it through different stages of a process. Notice how this user story does not describe a technology. In fact, if you think about it, there are a lot of solutions that could be used to solve this problem. The customer service representative could use a notepad on her desk and move the paper to a different stack to track it through the process. Of course, this is old fashioned, and we know the client wants to use Salesforce to solve her problem because she bought the licenses and here we are in a discovery session. But writing this way eliminates solutioning before it is time (see "Solutioning" in Chapter 9). Since the business process is distilled down to the who, what, and why, it creates flexibility and creativity for a solution architect to choose the best solution based on the constraints of the project. A solution architect will look at many user stories to determine the best solution for the project as a whole. And the Salesforce platform provides the architect with an array of "levers to pull" to craft a specific solution.

Acceptance Criteria

The second part of a user story is called the *acceptance criteria*. The acceptance criteria are testable scenarios that the solution must perform. Testable means that a person can test the scenario to see if it passes or not. The acceptance criteria is used by the QA engineer to write their test scripts and create traceability throughout the project.

When acceptance criteria are written using a special syntax called Gherkin, then the QA engineer can use this format to easily write their test scripts in a language called cucumber.io, which is used for automated test scripts. Automated testing is sometimes used on large projects. Instead of a user testing the functionality, a program runs through the scenario automatically and reports on if the script passed the test and is working as intended.

But even if you are not working on a project that has automated testing, Gherkin syntax is still a great format to use for acceptance criteria, because it helps the writer write a well-defined script that eliminates ambiguity. Gherkin is easy to write because it uses plain language. The statements are written using the template Given/When/Then. The statements can be strung together using AND to keep similar ideas together instead of creating a whole new story. Using the earlier example, the acceptance criteria could be written out like this:

Scenario: As a customer service representative, I want to record a customer interaction so that I can see it keep track of the issue until it is resolved.

Given I am interacting with a customer when I select an option to write and save my conversation, then my conversation will be there for future calls.

AND I can change the status of the record to either New, In Progress, Deferred, or Complete.

AND the date of the conversation will be saved.

Notice how this is testable. After this is built, someone can log in to the system as this persona and test that they can write a conversation, change the status, save it, and verify that the date is there. User stories are critical to help with planning and estimating the level of effort needed to complete a piece of functionality.

Team Cohesion

Before we move on to the development stage of a project, I think this is a good point to talk about team cohesion. Teams go through a predictable set of five stages of group development called the Tuckman model, named after Bruce Tuckman, an American psychological researcher who published the theory in 1965.[1] The five stages are forming, storming, norming, performing, and adjourning. Teams go through these stages at different rates.

By discovery, your team will have gone through the forming stage, which occurs when the team first comes together and is not yet working as a team. Introductions are made, and team members usually act polite to one another. People aren't quite sure what is going to happen on the project. People might be curious, confused, or anxious. The team will start testing the dependability of the leader in the group. The project manager plays a big role in this part of a project by being prepared, setting expectations, and making sure that everyone is aware of who is doing what on the project.

After forming comes storming. Don't be surprised if you start to feel the storming stage after discovery if not before. The storming stage is when team members naturally express their individuality and resist the formation of group structure. People start pushing against boundaries set by teammates. During storming your self-awareness is important. Nobody is going to tell you that storming has started. It is important to notice and identify it for what it is so that you can do something about it.

You will likely notice it if you pay attention. There could be interpersonal issues that arise between members of the team that cause division in the group. People may start stating their opinions, and this can cause agitation and

---

[1] Tuckman, W, Bruce, Psychological Bulletin, 1965, Vol 63, No. 6, pp 384–399, Retrieved 5/15/2021 https://web.mit.edu/curhan/www/docs/Articles/15341_Readings/Group_Dynamics/Tuckman_1965_Developmental_sequence_in_small_groups.pdf

conflicts to arise. There will be infighting and a lack of unity.[2] Or it can cause some people to shirk and let the stronger personality dominate. Some teams go through this phase slowly, and some go through it fast. Some teams never get past this stage, which makes for a stressful project. Some teams may think that they can avoid this phase, but it is best to acknowledge that this a natural step in forming a high-functioning team, and it is best to address any conflicts in the short term rather than letting them fester by ignoring them. See Chapter 10 for more tips on teamwork and how to get through this stage.

After the "storms" are over, the norming stage starts, where the team is in harmony. The project feels peaceful, and people start to really work together. The team togetherness and cohesion can be felt. On Salesforce Agile projects, I have found it is quite common for teams to experience norming during sprinting if not before. Sprinting has built-in ceremonies that establish norms. See Chapter 9 for more on sprinting.

Performing is when the team is working together as a unit with shared goals. They have put differences aside and are producing results. In my experience, working with a team that has achieved performance is exhilarating. Team members have a sense of accomplishment and togetherness that is a wonderful thing to be part of.

The fifth stage, adjourning, was added to Tuckman's model 12 years after the first four. Adjourning is a sad stage because it signifies the dissolution of the team where team members experience a sense of loss from after having established significant bonds with teammates.

Summary

Kickoff is the first meeting with a client during the discovery phase of a project. During this stage, the project team performs business analysis and examines the client's current and future business processes. Come to discovery with a curious mind so that you are open to learning new things. A member of the project team, usually the business analyst, will create process flows and well-formed user stories as project outputs or deliverables. The team will also begin the journey through the stages of group development, which include, forming, storming, norming, performing, and adjourning. Pay attention to the stage that your team is in so you can react accordingly.

---

[2] Tuckerman, https://web.mit.edu/curhan/www/docs/Articles/15341_Readings/
Group_Dynamics/Tuckman_1965_Developmental_sequence_in_small_groups.pdf

Resources

How to Build a Roadmap, `https://architect.salesforce.com/roadmap/roadmap-templates/how-to-roadmap/`

The Unified Modeling Language User Guide (2 ed.). Addison-Wesley. 2005. ISBN 0321267974

Gherkin syntax, `https://cucumber.io/docs/gherkin/reference/`

Mountain Goat Software, examples of how to write user stories and the general information on Agile, `https://www.mountaingoatsoftware.com/`

Build, Test, Deploy

The development or build, test, and deploy phases of a project are the parts of the project that contain several Agile ceremonies. Each ceremony contributes to the project structure and has purposes that if followed will help teams have a more successful project. The ceremonies include backlog refinement, sprint planning, and daily stand-ups and reviews.

The definition of ready and the definition of done are structured exercises that help align the team and create more efficiencies in work completion. Work cannot begin without a design. Overstating how important design is to project success is unlikely, so feel free to keep the solution design at the forefront of your mind when building an application and talk about it frequently so that the team is aligned and understands the big picture. The solution architect plays a critical role in making sure that the design for each user story fits into the overall solution design.

User acceptance testing is a time in the project when the end users test the system. It is important to conduct well-organized sessions with test scripts and to communicate expectations to end users. Scope creep is a risk during user acceptance testing but can be mitigated using traceability back to user stories and parsing through user feedback to determine if they may need training on a certain feature.

© Heather Negley 2022

H. Negley, *The Salesforce Consultant's Guide*,

https://doi.org/10.1007/978-1-4842-7960-1_9

Deployment is the end of a project when the application is moved to a production environment where end users interact with the system.

Agile Meetings

The official Agile ceremonies or Scrum events are sprint planning, daily scrum, sprint review, and sprint retrospective.[1] Backlog refinement is not an official Scrum ceremony, but it is a practice that works well with Scrum. It used to be called *backlog grooming* prior to 2013. Each Agile ceremony has its own meeting cadence.

Backlog Refinement

Once all the user stories are written, they are compiled into a list called a *backlog*. Backlog refinement is a prioritizing activity that goes hand in hand with the design of the application. The product owner is responsible for prioritizing the backlog. This means the product owner chooses which features will be built first. When the client is the product owner, then consultants can advise them with this prioritizing activity to help choose dependencies first and make suggestions based on their past experiences. Backlog refinement takes place throughout the project whenever there is a need to get more stories ready. Some teams have backlog refinement as often as twice a week during the build phase.

Each story is assigned an epic, which is a way to categorize the features. Sometimes epics are viewed as one large story that has been broken down into separate stories. In practicality, epics are useful because they help the team organize the stories, which is useful in prioritizing work.

Definition of Ready

Once all the stories are prioritized, they are ready and are pulled into sprints. But are they really ready? How does a team know? Creating a definition of ready helps; this is a list of rules that a story must meet in order for it to be considered for a sprint, and it helps eliminate ambiguity. How do you know what rules go into this? The team decides. The project team creates the definition of ready. You start by having a definition of ready meeting. Each project creates different rules, but the following are some common rules to consider:

---

[1] The Four Scrum Events and How to Use Them, https://resources.scrumalliance.org/Article/scrum-events

- Stories must have acceptance criteria.

- Stories larger than 21 points must be split before they are brought in.

- Stories must have a persona and an epic.

- All personas and epics must be written in a consistent manner to make filtering and sorting easier.

For example, backlog grooming may be held once or twice a week once sprinting has started to make sure the stories meet the definition of ready for sprint planning. Stories must earn their way to the top of the backlog.

An app always has a backlog with unfinished stories, unlike Waterfall where all requirements have to be completed by the end of the release.

Writing a backlog in a spreadsheet or ticketing software such as Jira are both popular ways that many companies use to manage their backlog. In Jira, epics are called *issues*. Also, epics may span multiple personas. See the "Visuals" section for more on how to show this in a visual way to clients.

Stories earn their way to the top of the backlog. Apps often have a backlog of stories that haven't earned their way into a release and stay in the backlog as ideas. Every app has a backlog. There is always a list of unfinished stories associated with an app. Stories must earn their way to the top. As time goes by and stories are deprioritized for certain releases, they may become stale or irrelevant because strategies have changed. So, it is normal for an app to have a list of stories that never make it out of the idea phase and sit in the backlog.

The product owner prioritizes stories by moving them to the top of the backlog. The team talks through the solution for the stories. It is a recurrent event.

Dependencies are important to identify from the project management level all the way down to the story level.

Design

Designing a solution goes hand in hand with backlog refinement because oftentimes in order to get the story to meet the definition of ready, more design discussions and decisions are needed. If a story doesn't have acceptance criteria, the solution architect and the stakeholders need to further refine the specific outcome that a user needs. Since acceptance criteria is written from a design-agnostic perspective, then a solution architect can create a design that meets the acceptance criteria or make sure the acceptance criteria is written in a way that fits into the overall design.

Tasking the story means writing out the exact configuration or coding steps so that the development team can build the app and meet the acceptance criteria. This isn't done in a vacuum story by story. The solution architect is looking at the solution as a whole to make this determination, looking at things from multiple perspectives such as license type, budget, scope, minimizing technical debt, and more.

One thing to note about license type is that purchased licenses grant access to different parts of the platform. Knowing what was purchased is a starting point for a solution architect. It goes a long way toward understanding the scope and the general direction of the project. A lot of Salesforce licenses have the word *cloud* in the name. Some popular clouds or licenses are Sales Cloud, Service Cloud, and Experience Cloud (formerly Community Cloud).[2]

Dependencies

A dependency is something that is blocking the start of something else. For example, if you are building a house, you must lay the foundation before you build the walls. A common dependency in a Salesforce project is establishing the data model, which is like a blueprint for the layout of a house. Setting up the data model needs to be done before you start configuring the fields on records and workflows and setting up the page layouts or user interface. The data model sets up the objects and their relationships to each other and is important to get right from the beginning. Rework to the data model is like removing a wall in a house after it has already been built. It can be done, but there are a lot of unintended consequences and risks than if you knew the wall shouldn't have been there in the beginning and just redid the blueprint. Changing record types, workflows, and layouts is like changing the paint on a wall, moving outlets around, and putting up trim and lighting. It is better for the whole design to incorporate dependencies in an elegant way instead of an after-the-fact patchwork.

Since a dependency needs to be completed first, it is harder to make changes to it once it is completed. This is why sometimes people add rooms to their houses. They can't go back and redo the entire layout of the house from scratch without a lot of time and effort. Systems that grow organically like this over time have extra customizations that weren't part of the original plan. They may work, but there may be technical debt from over-engineering that can lead to performance issues. It also complicates the design like how a Rube Goldberg machine is an overly complex design for completing a simple task or

---

[2] Explore the Complete Customer 360, https://www.salesforce.com/products/#products-scroll-tab, Retrieved on July 14, 2021.

how the Winchester Mystery House in San Jose, California, is so overly renovated from decades of rework by its eccentric owner, it is a popular tourist attraction.

Sprint Planning

Sprint planning is an Agile ceremony where the stories are selected for a sprint. Sprints are time boxes for completing a certain amount of work. A short project may have two or three sprints, while a longer project may have five or six sprints. An Agile project cannot have one sprint. That would make it a Waterfall project because it would lack iterative development and continuous feedback, which are two of the hallmarks of Agile.

Stories that meet the definition of ready are prioritized and selected for the sprint by the product owner. The Scrum master facilitates sprint planning. The level of effort of each story is also estimated. This is called *story pointing*.

Teams may estimate stories together as a group. One popular way to do this is with an activity known as Planning Poker or Scrum Poker. It is a gamified way for teams to estimate a backlog and is derived from the Wideband Delphi estimation method that was developed by the RAND Corporation in the 1950s.

When a team "points" a story, they assign it an estimate of the amount of effort it takes to complete a story. It is not supposed to be a measure of time. However, it is quite common for clients to mistake story points for time estimates.

Two common ways to assign story points is by using T-shirt sizes or a Fibonacci sequence. Using T-shirt sizes, a story may be assigned S, M, L or XL for a small, medium, large, or extra-large level of effort. A Fibonacci sequence is a fun mathematics formula where each number in the sequence is the sum of two numbers that precedes it. 0, 1, 1, 2, 3, 5, 8, 13, 21, 34...etc. For example, a small level of effort story would be a one-point story, and a 21-point story may be too much effort to even bring into a sprint and would need to be split up into smaller stories. A Fibonacci sequence is also a naturally occurring pattern in nature as sometimes referred to as the Golden Ratio (see Figure 9-1).

Figure 9-1. Seashell with a Fibonnaci spiral sequence

Velocity is a measure of how many story points a team can complete in a sprint. Project managers keep track of this to help gauge the amount of work a team can complete in a sprint. Velocity usually goes up as teams get used to working together and norms are established.

Definition of Done

The definition of done is a list of criteria that a story must meet in order to be considered finished. Like the definition of ready, the list is different for every Scrum team. Here are some common examples:

1. The story needs to be unit tested, which means that someone on the team needs to make sure to check the developer's work. This is different than the user acceptance testing, which is at the end of sprinting and is where the users test the functionality.

2. Code review passed.

3. Deployed to next environment.

4. Demo completed, but not tested and accepted by end users (user acceptance testing) or deployed to production.

Sprinting

Sprints are blocks of time where development work is done. They have milestones and Agile ceremonies to give the team structure to support an iterative build and get continuous feedback.

Daily Stand- Ups

Daily upstand-ups are an Agile ceremony occurring every day in order for the team to brief one another. It is a self-organizing meeting, meaning that the project manager and/or Scrum master does not have to run it for the team.

The stand-up is a short meeting of around 15 minutes or less where each team member reports what they are working on and if they have any blockers. Three basic questions are usually answered by each team member.

- What was done yesterday?
- What will be done today?
- What are the blockers?

A blocker is another way of saying that work on a specific task cannot proceed. There are many reasons for this, and the Scrum master or project manager plays an important role in helping team members unblock their issues. Sometimes individuals need to talk after the stand-up to discuss issues in more detail.

The Scrum board may also be displayed to show the progress the stories are making. It is important for team members to keep their stories updated. Figure 9-2 is an example of a Scrum board and shows how a team works together to track the progress of development work. Some teams use Scrum boards in Jira, while others may have paper boards on sticky notes in person.

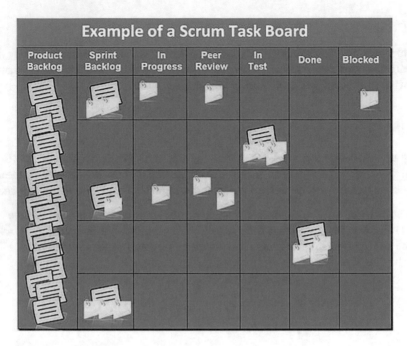

Figure 9-2. Example of a Scrum board

Identifying Risks and Issues

Risks and issues are identified all through the project. The whole team should look for them. A risk is something that hasn't happened yet but may happen. An issue is a problem that has materialized and needs to be mitigated.

It is common for new risks and issues to emerge during sprinting because of all the work being done. It is impossible to predict everything that may happen beforehand, so when development starts, raising new risks and issues quickly is important for team success. The project manager will keep a risk and issue log and help the team manage them until they are solved or accepted.

On a Salesforce project, an example of accepted risk could be a risk where a client computer needs to be shipped to a consultant before they can log into Salesforce. There could be mitigations for this risk such as asking the client to send the computer overnight to save time, or the project manager may accept this risk because it falls within a tolerated level of risk.

Two common pitfalls to be aware of include regarding risks and issues are as follows:

- Inaction when action is needed
- Inaccurate assumptions

Raising an issue is the first step to solving a problem. An issue needs a mitigation plan to help solve it. Sometimes this means escalating the issue to project leaders and communicating the impact that the issue is having on the project. Then it is important to have a conversation about possible actions to take to solve the problem. Passivity is not the best way to manage risks and issues and can lead to confusion and revisionist history. Revisionist history is when people make untrue statements about events that occurred in the past. Documenting and working on risk and issues on a regular basis is the best way to avoid this.

It is also important to communicate your assumptions around a problem. People may arrive at different conclusions because they are assuming different things. It is important to state what you have assumed in order to arrive at your conclusion. Many times the differing perspective is at the assumption level, and it is much clearer to have a conversation around differing assumptions rather than a multitude of differing conclusions. For example, if you write a report based on the assumption that the information that you need to draw your conclusions are in the statement of work, then you can make a note of that in the report under the assumptions section. You may find that everyone is in agreement, or you may find that the client wants you to write your report from the perspective of everything they have told you over the last six weeks whether or not it is in the statement of work. If you write your report this way, then you will wind up with a much different report. But either way, it is still important that you state your assumptions in the report.

Sprint Reviews

A sprint review is an Agile ceremony run by the business analyst and is an exciting time for a project team to demonstrate the up-to-date functionality that has been completed and to receive feedback. Sprint reviews are important because they validate the direction the team is going and can also help the team make adjustments so that everyone is aligned. Demos are one of the ways that continuous feedback is achieved.

Demo Tips

Here are some tips for the demo:

- **Prepare**. Create test accounts, test users, and any other test data that you need for your demo ahead of time. Creating a presentation with the scenarios that you are going to show to help give your audience context and lead them from a conceptual stage to a built-out feature in the system.

- **Rehearse**. Rehearsal is a useful metacognition strategy, which means to think about your thinking. Rehearsing for a demo helps you master your internal language and thinking. Just because you plan it out in your head doesn't mean it will sound the same way when you say your thoughts out loud. Create an outline and write down a couple of key points that you want to cover. Practice paraphrasing instead of reading your notes word for word. You want to sound fluent when you say your thoughts out loud and not stilted.

- **Present**. At the beginning, tell the audience what you are going to present. Present it and then tell them what you presented.

- **Don't point out mistakes**. There may be mistakes in the demo, which is okay. Don't be thrown off or overly apologetic by them. You may be focusing on minor issues that are not even obvious to the audience. Ideally, your rehearsal will have caught major issues. Even if something unexpected does happen, try to go with the flow and focus on what is working and what is interesting and what progress has been made. A system during this stage of development has not been fully tested, so bugs are likely. The goal is to communicate the general direction of the build and what has been accomplished. The demo isn't supposed to be the core purpose of a sprint review although sometimes it does take center stage.

- **Ask for feedback**. Ask the audience if the update is what they were envisioning for this sprint.

- **Ask the product owner to accept the stories**. After feedback has been collected, ask the product owner to formally accept the stories so they can be closed out and preparations for the next sprint can begin. If the product owner does not accept a story, then it must be prioritized for the next sprint. Most likely it will be moved to the next sprint, but it is possible that the product owner wants to deprioritize it.

Retrospective

The retrospective is an Agile ceremony used to evaluate the project and reflect on the sprint. There are common templates that are used for this ceremony that center around the identifying activities that the team wants to turn into norms that activities that the team wants to eliminate.

The following are common questions during a retrospective:

- What went well
- What didn't go well
- What you want to repeat
- What you want to stop

Visuals

Visuals can work wonders to better communicate complex or confusing concepts. In addition to the visuals used in discovery that we have reviewed such as the process workflow and a RACI, there are many more that can be used throughout the project. Visuals are useful when communicating complex concepts. It takes longer to teach someone a complex concept using words alone. There is only so much information that people can hold in their head while trying to learn something new. Oftentimes, people lose the thread of information, especially if it gets too long and forks off in different branches with different logical considerations. Once you go down several branches of logic and discuss the possibilities, it is hard to keep up with everything that was covered. Visuals help with this.

Work Breakdown Structure

A work breakdown structure is a visual representation of the work to be completed. Sometimes this term is used in project management and is synonymous with project plan, but in this context, it is a visual that shows the content of the work that is to be completed and not the milestones in a project. It helps to visualize a backlog. For example, If you are working on a project with many personas and epics, creating a work breakdown structure is useful. Figure 9-3 depicts the personas across the top row with the epics underneath.

Figure 9-3. Personas and epics

User Acceptance Testing

At the end of build, the end user gets a chance to test the functionality themselves. This event is called *user acceptance testing*. Test scripts written from the acceptance criteria in the user stories are used by testers to test the system in a methodological way. This structure also ensures proper traceability is maintained throughout the stages of the project. By the time a test script gets in the hands of a tester, the tester has to report their findings. If they question why a piece of functionality is working a certain way, then the team can trace the functionality in question back to the user story.

There are three possible outcomes to a test script. They are defects, training, or new ideas. A defect is reported if the test does not pass and the functionality works differently than what the expected behavior is, which is also explained in the test script. Defects are also called bugs, which is an old term that was coined by Thomas Edison, but in 1947 computer science engineer Admiral Grace Hopper was helping a colleague troubleshoot a malfunctioning computer when she found an actual bug in it (Figure 9-4).[3]

---

[3] Atlas Obsura, https://www.atlasobscura.com/places/grace-hoppers-bug, Retrieved on 8/28/2021

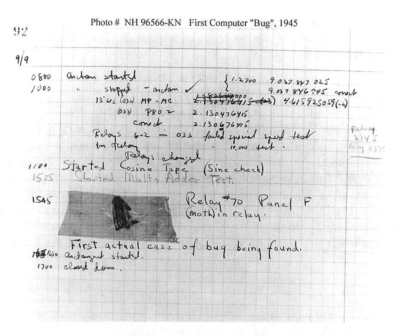

Figure 9-4. Photo of first computer bug (Source: US Navy, Naval Surface Warfare Center, Dahlgren Division, Public Domain, Atlas Obsura, https:// www.atlasobscura.com/places/ grace-hoppers-bug, retrieved on 8/28/2021)

Training on the implementation also takes place at the end of the build phase usually after user acceptance testing. Sometimes the consultants teach Train the Trainer and Admin sessions so that trainers can teach users in the company how to and administer the system. These are usually not Salesforce training sessions that teach end users in-depth features of Salesforce as if they were training to become experts. The training is more end user focused with the aim of teaching stakeholders how to do their jobs using the system.

Deployment

In software development, the end of the project is when the software is put into use or deployed. Sometimes this is called the *release*. Project managers plan release schedules with clients so that certain pieces of functionality are released in a given time frame that is preplanned.

Deployment means to make the application work in the appropriate environment. During a project, the application moves from one environment to the next depending on the stage of the project. For example, during the build phase, the application is built in the development environment. Then during UAT the application is moved to the UAT environment. Then when it is ready for the end user to start using, it is moved to the production environment, which is considered the "live" environment. Some projects may have a more complex environment plan with more environments to manage other risks with release managers who are responsible for ensuring the release plan is followed accordingly.

Summary

There are several Agile meetings that create structure in a project. They include backlog refinement, sprint planning, daily stand-ups, sprint reviews, and retrospectives. Visuals should be used to help clients conceptualize complex logic. User acceptance testing is a chance for end users to test the system that gives feedback. Remember to conduct well-organized user acceptance sessions. Mitigate the risk of scope creep by identifying enhancements for future phases and training items. Deployment is the end of the project when the application is moved to the production environment.

Resources

Winchester Mystery House, a house that was continually renovated for 36 years, `https://www.winchestermysteryhouse.com/`

Planning Poker, a paid digital version of the Agile planning tool for virtual teams, `https://www.planningpoker.com/`

Consulting Skills

Client Management

As a Salesforce consultant, you will need refined soft skills in order to help clients achieve project success. Practicing soft skills or consulting skills is something that is never complete. The more you practice them, the better you become. Important soft skills for Salesforce consulting include client management, communication, emotional intelligence, and critical thinking. These skills are so important that I am dedicating a chapter for each one.

In this chapter, I will begin with an overview of soft skills followed by a way to approach client management through identifying patterns. I have developed archetypes for predictable patterns that I have encountered in my experience working on Salesforce projects. The subsequent chapters focus on specific soft skills and strategies, including key times in the project or situation to utilize a particular skill.

There are a few predictable patterns that can emerge in projects that when identified can be aided with soft skills. Identifying these patterns through the archetypes presented in the chapter can help you identify and utilize the correct soft skill needed to manage the client.

© Heather Negley 2022
H. Negley, *The Salesforce Consultant's Guide*,
https://doi.org/10.1007/978-1-4842-7960-1_10

What Are Soft Skills?

Salesforce consultants need more than technical skills to be effective. There are a collection of nonfunctional or soft skills that are needed for effective projects including but not limited to client management, communication, emotional awareness, and critical thinking. Be aware that these skills are not technical, but they are critical to becoming a successful Salesforce consultant. Technologies are always changing, and new technical certifications are always emerging. Soft skills don't change, but they need practice. They are best when they are refined over and over with time and experience.

According to a 2021 workplace effectiveness study, one of the biggest barriers in the workplace is employee emotions or psychological commitment due to organizational factors. These factors include, in part, leaders, co-workers, bureaucracy, process, and implementation issues.[1] Having the soft skills to effectively work with clients is necessary.

Project Archetypes

Client management is an important soft skill to practice in Salesforce consulting. Since Salesforce consulting is project-based work, it is paramount to understand client behavior and patterns in the context of a project. Depending on the circumstances, Salesforce projects may follow a predictable pattern of behavior. To make this easier for you, I have named the patterns of behavior that I have observed from my experience on dozens of Salesforce projects. If you can identify a pattern, then you can map it to one of the archetypes in this section. Not all patterns are bad. They help you figure out which consulting tool in your toolbox to use for a given situation. To borrow an old saying, when all you have is a hammer, everything requires a nail. I want to teach you that every project is unique and to give you more than just a hammer to solve issues. Also, don't be surprised if you see two or three archetypes in your project. Salesforce projects are dynamic. There is always a different mix of people and technologies. Even time changes the dynamic. A project done four years ago will look different if done again tomorrow.

The Hydra

A hydra is a multiple-headed serpent from Greek mythology (see Figure 10-1). Hydra projects are projects with a split power base (they're "multiheaded"). For example, usually projects have one executive sponsor who is in charge of communicating the vision and strategy, but on occasion, you may find projects

---

[1] Understanding Barriers in the Workplace, LivingBluPrints, 2021 White Paper, https://checkout.square.site/buy/E3H2OOG7D5VQ2VYFDFTVJIML

with more than one executive sponsor. This causes projects to behave like a hydra. For example, one head may give directions that conflict with the other head. One head could be from the business side of the organization and the other head from the technology side. This can be problematic if you are the consultant, because you may receive directions that align with one head but then have a contradictory conversation with the other head. Since both heads are in charge, this creates chaos, confusion, and swirling conversations. This swirl creates inertia and causes timeline slippage, which naturally delays the project.

Figure 10-1. A hydra: from Greek mythology, a serpent with many heads

Watch Out For

- Inertia

- Conversation swirl

- Scavenger hunts

- Schedule delays and budget overruns

Communication swirl is the most common side effect in a hydra, so if you notice it, you may want to ask yourself if the swirl is being created when one group communicates to you from one decision-making point of view and then another person in a position of power contradicts the first person, and then it loops back and forth. Communication swirl can happen in other project archetypes, but on a hydra project, the swirl is being created by the multiple heads.

To be fair, from an organizational point of view, there may be good reasons that responsibilities are divided between heads. Perhaps they share the budget for the project. But from a decision-making perspective regarding project strategy and execution, this model doesn't translate effectively.

Please also beware of scavenger hunts on hydra projects because there is a risk of too many uncoordinated, free-agent stakeholders. They can emerge as a result of continual conversation and a misaligned strategy. Hydra heads with disparate and distinct strategies for a project may send project members on scavenger hunts to gather and analyze information to help prove their point of view. Some requests may help align the two heads, while others may be requests for scenarios that are edge cases or scenarios that are completely out of scope. Depending on the timeline, extensive research and analysis on what-if scenarios can turn into scavenger hunts that may have no impact on the current project except to waste time. Beware of circular, repetitive, and spiraling conversations with no resolution and tangents that dig into details that lead the team farther and farther away from the main goal.

Strategies to Help

- Internal committee formations
- Timebox research and analysis requests
- Proofs of concepts

Don't keep on going around and around from one contradictory conversation to the next for an extended period of time. Once you identify it is happening, then try to stop it. One way to do this on a hydra project is to determine if there is a lack of coordination and communication between the multiple heads. Ask yourself if you are hearing two distinct and separate goals from them that are at odds with one another. To help the client form consensus, suggest that they form an internal committee to align internally so that they can communicate one vision and strategy to you and your team. Sometimes clients create decision-making committees and assign a person such as the product owner to communicate one message that the whole group agrees on. Many times, this is the first time these separate groups have come together to talk about the matters at hand, and it is time well spent.

Timebox research and analysis requests to avoid scavenger hunts on hydra projects. If the swirl and scavenger hunt requests continue unabated and the groups cannot align, then a proof of concept is another tool in your toolbox that may help get the project back on track. The client may want to see what one of their ideas will look like in Salesforce with their own data, fields, page layouts, and reports and dashboards. This type of exercise is called a *proof of concept* and is considered a separate effort from a traditional delivery project. Many times, people are able to understand linear concepts through a visual proof of concept easier than talking about it and looking at process flow and data diagrams. A proof of concept is a small sample project used to communicate a concept in context and is very effective for visual people. A small sample of the requirements are used to build an example of what the application would look like in a project. A proof of concept is similar to a demonstration at the end of a sprint but comes before a delivery project starts.

If a client asks for a proof of concept, then consider it a separate project that requires a change order. If the project is big enough, it may be worth it to the client to spend the extra money to make sure they will be getting something that they want. I have seen proof of concepts unstick hydra projects and help their organization quickly decide on a design after months of inertia.

The Echo Chamber

The echo chamber is a project that does not have any client-side stakeholders or has stakeholders with limited time. At the beginning of a project, consultants ask for regular employee participation during kickoff and discovery and other key meetings. This is so the project will have a greater chance at success. But by doing so, it takes people away from their regular jobs. Unless their supervisors have alleviated their responsibilities, they may have a hard time dedicating themselves to the project and juggling the extra responsibilities. This is especially true for the product owner who needs to dedicate more of their time to the project than other project stakeholders. A project with limited stakeholder participation creates a void that lacks ideas and solutions and merely echoes back a lone voice or two. It also creates a major project risk of the project team not receiving sign-off on the project from the client.

Watch Out For

- Unresponsiveness and lack of engagement
- Pushback
- Lack of accountability
- Last-minute changes
- Poor user adoption

Clients on an echo chamber project are usually overwhelmed from having to do two jobs, so they may use coping mechanisms to buy themselves more time or avoid accountability. Sometimes these behaviors may not be conscious deflections. But it is important for you as the consultant to recognize these behaviors when you see them so that you can select the right tool in your toolbox to manage the issue.

A common coping mechanism from someone who feels overwhelmed or cornered because they have been assigned too much work is unresponsiveness to meeting invites or sporadic acceptance of invitations. If this person is a decision-maker, escalate this quickly because they may swoop in at the end of UAT and throw the project into a tailspin with last-minute changes. Last-minute requests from someone who has not participated in the project are especially destructive, because the person making these requests often lacks context of prior decisions made by the project team. It may take time to get the person up to speed and read into the project, but if they are demanding changes without knowing the design or other key decisions, then they could cause a schedule delay.

Other coping behaviors include stakeholders who act clueless or passive when asked for information. They may push back and refuse to accept responsibility or deflect by saying that they aren't the right person to answer the specific question. This is a way to avoid accountability.

Strategies to Help

- RACI
- Escalate proactively and quickly
- Ask for more resources
- Hold monthly executive meetings

If you find yourself in an echo chamber project, it is important to act proactively to set expectations with the client. It is good to anticipate what might need to be done next instead of passively waiting for the right people to show up. Passivity ultimately leads to a breakdown in communication and project delays. If a key stakeholder is not participating in the project on a daily basis, then escalate this issue to your manager.

There are quite a few tools to use to mitigate risks on an echo chamber project. One thing to do right away is to create a RACI (see Chapter 7) so that all the stakeholders know their roles and expectations. Define who is accountable. Ask that accountable team members be involved in the project and attend key meetings. Escalate issues to your project manager if they do not participate.

Another tool from your toolbox in an echo chamber project is to suggest that the employees receive relief from their other responsibilities to dedicate time to the project. After all, the company has already made the decision to purchase Salesforce consulting services, so it is in their best interest to get the most for their money. Allocating resource time to the project is a good way to ensure value. It is also a good practice to conduct monthly executive meetings for people who are not participating in the project on a daily basis. It is important to obtain a sign-off before moving forward. It is a common mistake to keep moving forward just so you are doing something. This creates an illusion of progress from the burning budget, but if all stakeholders are not aligned, then it is a risk to the project.

Poor user adoption is a common outcome of echo chamber projects. You can mitigate this by having change management activities incorporated into the project. For example, find power users who can serve as change champions for other users. Work the client side to help them create a change management schedule for rolling out the new application and communicating key milestones to users.

Swiss Cheese

A Swiss cheese project is full of holes similar to blind spots. In other words, they are projects where key information is missing. Overall, this missing information creates a partial, unfinished perspective of the project.

You will know if you are on a Swiss cheese project if you cannot get answers to major information gathering questions. The five Ws often used in journalism are who, what, when, where, and why. If you can't answer all five, then there is a blind spot on the project. Here is an example of how the five Ws could look on a Salesforce project:

- Who are the stakeholders? Who is on the project team? Who is the product owner? Who is managing the project?

- What is the scope of the project? What is the timeline? What is the budget? What is the vision? What are the goals? What problem does this project solve? What is the business value that will come from this project? What are the current processes? What are the current technologies?

- When is the application due? When is the application going to launch in production? When is user acceptance testing?

- Where the kickoff going to be held? Where are the Salesforce environments? Where is the project going to take place? Where are the key stakeholders located?

- Why is the company doing the project?

- How does this project fit into the overall strategy of the company in terms of goals and key performance indicators? How is the data organized?

These projects can have many stakeholders or very few. The important thing is for someone on the project to understand and communicate the answer to all your particular five W questions until the team is aligned. The answers might not all come from one person. But the team should keep on asking until all the blind spots are erased with a clear answer.

Watch Out For

- Answers to key five Ws missing from project

- Lack of engagement

- Poor user adoption

Strategies to Help

Keep asking the five W questions to every new person who joins the project. Give homework out to stakeholders for any unanswered W question. If there is a lack of engagement, then use tools from the echo chamber project.

The Explorer

Working on explorer projects is great fun because these are projects where the client likes to learn and is deeply engaged. On explorer projects, the stakeholders gain an understanding of the power of workflow automation. It can be a transformational experience to show someone how to go from a manual-based process such as paper or email to the first, small steps of an automated environment. It usually opens up the creative mind and a plethora of possibilities for tracking business intelligence. It is fun to watch someone make this realization for the first time.

As a consultant, it feels a little like guiding someone up a hiking trail to the top of a mountain. It is harder to explain the view from the top unless they see it themselves. The same goes for understanding automation for the first time. In the beginning, you may have to teach the basics of automation such as the concept of statuses and how fields can trigger actions in the database. You have to lead them up the path of understanding a minimum amount so they can see the view at the top to see what is possible. Once they get there, the possibilities do seem endless. Again your role is to make sure your client doesn't start running off in a million directions at once. Ideas are exciting but at a pace. This is the heart of the Crawl, Walk, Run approach that I discussed in Chapter 4.

Watch Out For

- Scope creep
- Rabbit holes
- Schedule slippage

Manage scope creep when ideas get out of hand. Talk about the long view. Don't get stuck in detailed unrelated analysis or rabbit holes in the middle of a project. Remind the client of the current timeline monitor risks and issues that may delay the project.

Strategies to Help

Explorer projects can become fast moving with all the ideas flowing. Stakeholders like to explore new options and scenarios. It is important to take the time to teach them about the evolution of automating an application. Workforce automation is a gradual process. It requires a slower start with a ramp-up to make decisions at key points. While it is an exciting time to automate manual processes, not everything needs to be automated at once. Teach your client to start with a minimum viable product (MVP) to pace the vision. Work to come to an agreement on parts or the minimum features required to create an application for the current release.

Help the client think through the phases of automating and make a plan to proceed at a sustainable pace. Teach them about the Crawl, Walk, Run approach. Then plan subsequent releases or a roadmap to look ahead and incorporate more and more automation, business intelligence such as predictive analytics, artificial intelligence, and more.

Teach that at first it may make more sense to leave some tasks in the system as user initiated based on decisions they need to make at certain times rather than thinking of every permutation that can trigger a system to send a notification, change a status or field, and set off another workflow. Human decisions are still important. Some things still require a human to make a judgment call, especially things with a high degree of variability. If there are such decisions, then recommend they start with a manual entry in key areas to leave room for human monitoring and decision-making.

The Rube Goldberg

Let's face it, Rube Goldberg machines are fun to watch because of the creativity run amuck. The self-operating napkin in Figure 10-2 would be fun to watch if it really worked. Of course, it is not something that you actually want to build because it is highly inefficient. On a Salesforce project, over-customization of an application can lead to Rube Goldberg type of solutions that create high technical debt and poor scalability. They usually come about from scope creep, which turns into overly complex designs. For example, an explorer can easily turn into a Rube Goldberg project if not properly paced and planned out.

Figure 10-2. By Rube Goldberg, originally published in Collier's, September 26, 1931, Public Domain, https://commons.wikimedia.org/w/index.php?curid=9886955

Watch Out For

- Scope creep
- Rabbit holes
- Over-engineering
- Technical debt

Strategies to Help

If you are staffed on a project to develop an application in an existing org, it is important to be aware of the level of technical debt that exists in that org. When an org has high technical tech, it may be riskier for your project team to successfully deliver your implementation. High technical debt means that the code was written in such a way that makes it hard to modify in the future. Mitigating this type of delivery risk is important to achieve project success.

One way to determine the level of technical debt is with a health check. And it may be a good way to start your project. Health checks are analytical efforts that check for performance issues and make suggestions for technical modifications to remove complexity and customization so that the org does not operate on the threshold of system limits.

If you are working in a new org and you find the project entering into scope creep and rabbit hole territory, try to manage these issues so that the org does not become over-engineered and turn into a Rube Goldberg machine. Utilize strategies such as the MVP and Crawl, Walk, Run as discussed in the explorer project to mitigate these risks. Focus on the design, the roadmap, and the system architecture in the company as a whole. Here are questions to ask the team:

- Would adding this requirement make the solution overly complex?
- Is this feature better off somewhere else?
- How could it fit into a systems design plan?
- Do we need to redesign or refactor the existing code or proposal? Don't get stuck with a sunk cost fallacy with endless patches instead of a redesign.

High Horse

High horse projects are projects that are dictated by one person. They aren't really team projects. The distribution of power is lopsided. This person can be on the client side. Sometimes they are on your team. These projects become dysfunctional quickly because one person with power does all the talking and doesn't listen. This is not the same thing as a project sponsor who has a vision. This is a person who avoids accountability but exerts power over the team.

Watch Out For

- Conversation swirl
- Revisionist history
- Misaligned expectations
- Rework, rework, rework

Like on a hydra project, disorienting conversation that swirls around from one topic to the next without resolution is common on a high horse project.

Best-practice recommendations become thwarted by leaders on high horse projects. Changes lead to rework, which lead to revisionist histories and misaligned expectations.

Strategies to Help

Manage risk and issues tightly. Work and rework mitigations. Record decisions. Keep a conversation log. Memories are short on these types of projects. You might have to go back in your logs to remember what was discussed a few days or weeks earlier. Memories are short, and written logs and documentation are important to remind the team of conversations and decisions made in the past. Revisionist history is common if people forget past conversations. Another approach is to try to build their confidence in you by demonstrating expertise.

Most important, escalations are important to do on high horse projects because they cause all kinds of risks and issues. Persuasion techniques and logic arguments may seem effective at first but often result in gaslighting techniques after the fact. If you find yourself on a high horse project, try to remind yourself that not all projects are like this and see if there is anything you can learn from the situation. Sometimes the worst projects teach you the most.

Stick in the Mud

A stick in the mud is a project that is not moving along through the project stages at a normal gait. It is stuck. These projects can have stakeholders who are resistant to change or who can't agree on important decisions. They are slow-moving projects with just a handful of stakeholders and low adoption rates for the organization. This is different from an echo chamber project where the stakeholders don't have enough time to participate, though they do have some similarities such as lack of engagement and poor user adoption. Stick in the mud projects are distinctively different because the stakeholders refuse to participate.

For example, I once was on a project for a large organization where the client gave the business stakeholders the option of whether they wanted to participate. One of my responsibilities was to walk around the campus asking different departments if they wanted to participate. Everyone said "no." The way they saw it was "If it ain't broke, why fix it." Nobody wanted to change the way they were working even if their technology and processes were outdated. They saw no reason to change. It was more work to change. And the project sponsor did not have the power to mandate the change.

Leaving it optional may get very little participation from people who are happy with the way things have been going for them and see no reason to change the way they work.

Watch Out For

- No buy-in from client stakeholders
- Poor user adoption
- Lack of mandate or incentive
- Schedule slippage

Strategies to Help

- Change Management
- Incentives

Most projects need some degree of change management to have sufficient user adoption because of the very nature of creating something new. But stick in the mud projects need change management the most. If you don't have stakeholders on the project, you have a problem. If you can't mandate participation, then incentivizing people with games or prizes is another option.

Summary

Client management is an important soft skill. Identifying patterns in projects is key in helping you identify the consulting tools you need to utilize to effectively help your client. From hydras to high horses, there really is no such thing as a perfect project, but that's what makes them interesting. Building applications is a fulfilling endeavor. Just remember, a fun explorer project can turn into a Rube Goldberg if you don't manage the client and let ideas run wildly away. A stick in the mud is similar to an echo chamber but with no stakeholders. And a Swiss cheese project may feel surreal, but search for answers. Don't accept the holes. Gather information until you can see the big picture.

Resource

Crawl Walk Run, https://www.salesforce.org/blog/crawl-walk-run-salesforce-implementation-guide/

Communication

Besides the willingness to learn, knowing how to effectively communicate is the most important skill to possess as a Salesforce consultant Choosing a communication method is such an important aspect to what we do in our lives that taking the time to select the right medium is critical to effectively communicate. You have to be willing to really listen in order to exchange meaningful messages to teach and learn from one another. It is a mutual exchange. Public speaking and writing are other key elements to master. Slack is a new way to communicate at work and is an important medium to understand.

The Medium Is the Message

"The medium is the message" is a famous phrase coined by Marshall McLellan in 1964. It is a profound quote and has long been a favorite of mine, because it distills the importance of thinking about the medium you choose when communicating. McLellan meant that understanding the character of the medium is as important as the message itself. As a Salesforce consultant, selecting the medium in which to communicate a message to your team and client is more important than you may first realize.

McLellan explained, "Indeed, it is only too typical that the content of any medium binds up to the character of the medium."[1] This means that the

---

[1] McLuhan, Marshall (1964). *Understanding Media: The Extensions of Man*. ISBN 81-14-67535-7.

© Heather Negley 2022
H. Negley, *The Salesforce Consultant's Guide*,
https://doi.org/10.1007/978-1-4842-7960-1_11

message itself is restrained and organized by the medium in which it passes. He proffered a lightbulb as an example of a medium without a message. The bulb in itself is a medium. The electric light is pure information that passes through the lightbulb; however, there is no actual message being transmitted. Yet the medium that is the bulb still has an effect on us. The bulb creates light, which helps people create spaces at night, a time that would otherwise be dark. The light bulb is an example of a technology that changes society's norms and values.

When you think about it, the invention of new communication technologies have redesigned and refined societal norms and values over and over again, from the radio to television, from the landline rotary phone to the smartphone, from the Pony Express to social media, from email to texting. These media establish a structure or arrangement for our awareness. And they all do it with a unique flair. Each one commands our attention in a different way. With this in mind, when you work on a project, take a moment to think through your media selection so that you select the appropriate structure for your message to live in. Think about how big the impression will be on the receiver with just the media selection alone before anything is even communicated.

What does it say if you pick up the phone to call someone versus sending an email? Choosing your medium is as important as the message. For example, when your phone rings and you answer it, how alert are you during that moment after you say "hello" and are waiting for a response from the person? How much attention are you generating compared to reading a message in your feed? This is a difference with the amount of attention given to the medium.

Another example is Twitter, which is used for efficiency for people who want to discover something new quickly. Messages are limited in length the same way telegraph messages were limited and used for signaling. The average-length telegrams of the 1900s were around 11 words long.[2] So, whether you choose a phone, slide deck presentation, conference call, text, email, or some other medium, be aware of not only the message but also the medium. Choose wisely.

Listening

To listen well is an art of sorts. There needs to be a focus and a willingness to take new information into an empty space in your mind. It takes some practice to not speak when that first thought pops into your head when you listen.

---

[2] Hochfelder, David (2012). *The Telegraph in America, 1832–1920*. The Johns Hopkins University Press. p. 79. ISBN 9781421407470.

Have you ever looked at a person while they were talking but were really paying attention to your own thoughts? This isn't listening. This is thinking and pretending to listen. Listening may appear passive, but it is not. To listen fully is to focus and direct your attention to the speaker and filter out other noises, thoughts, and distractions with a goal of seeing things from another person's point of view.

When you focus on an empty space in your mind, there is a suspension of animation. Each new piece of information that enters a mind in this state will percolate if you let it. If you let it strain through your senses and don't react to it right away, then you are listening. You must engage your senses to listen. Not just your ears. Your eyes also pick up nonverbal body language, and perhaps the smells around you contribute as well. Touch certainly does. Sound makes vibrations that can be felt. All these senses contribute to decoding the message.

Taking the information in is only one part. One must also learn how to communicate back. There are many ways to do this. Maintain good eye contact and nod, but also say something that validates that you heard them. Simply repeating back their own sentence to them works. And say the speaker's name. People love the sound of their own name. But be authentic. It is not formulaic. Remember, it is an art. Listening is not complicated. It is not fast. It is not frenetic and not a transaction. It is more Zen. It is smooth with curved lines that drop in an echo chamber that collects into an amorphous shape that is shared back and transformed into full communication.

Speaking and Writing

Sometimes choosing the right word can make all the difference. Subtlety can go a long way, and even well-placed silence has a powerful effect instead of filling every minute with words. Pay attention to the words you select. For example, do you ever use the words "I just" when you are speaking or even writing an email, as in "it's just me"? Drop the "just." It diminishes your message and your power. You may use it because you may feel like you are intruding on someone's time, and it's a way of saying "excuse me." But your message is better without it.

Two other common phrases that people often use interchangeably are "I think" and "I feel." You may be using one automatically and not even realize it. Use both. But make a conscious decision when using them. Choose "I think" to communicate a thought and "I feel" for emotions. You may have to analyze what you want to communicate. Do you want to communicate a feeling? If so, that's fine. Humans have both thoughts and feelings. Just be sure that is what you mean. "I feel good about this" and "I think this is a good idea" are two different messages. You can think something is a good idea and feel bad about it. Word choice is important.

Word choices also help when delivering messages that are hard. For example, instead of telling a client that their idea doesn't make sense and is not practical or a best practice, use the word "unconventional" as in "That data solution is unconventional." This is nearly a compliment and suggests creativity. And if you are on a Rube Goldberg project, this is probably really what you mean.

Also, repeating what you think you heard back to the person you are talking to helps. Try saying, "Let me see if I understand what you said" and then repeat back what they said. This type of clarification strategy helps make sure that messages have been effectively communicated.

Public Speaking

As a Salesforce consultant, you will have to get comfortable doing a fair amount of public speaking. The audiences may not always be enormous, but you should be comfortable leading a session for 20+ people.

The more public speaking that you do, the better you will become. Trailhead has a Public Speaking Skills module that can help you plan and find opportunities to practice presenting. See the "Resources" section.

Slack

Slack is a whole new way for people at work to talk to each other. It brings our personal and work lives closer together. Slack is an app that uses workspaces and channels for conversations.

I first encountered Slack in 2016, when I was working for a consulting company that used it as their internal chatting service. Some of the channels were project related, and others were a jokey type of communication that you would normally have in the lunchroom. I was fascinated by this since the majority of the company was remote and didn't meet in an actual lunchroom.

One of the most interesting aspects of Slack is the stream-of-consciousness, immediate communication you can do with emojis for any occurrence you can think of. I'll never forget the first time I saw the screaming head emoji pop up in the middle of a meeting with the client. We were on a conference call, and the client said something that triggered the solution architect who sent me a message that just said "no" followed by the scream emoji. I really understood Slack as a medium at that moment. I got the "secret sauce" of the medium. It was allowing people to communicate their emotions at work during a meeting in real time. I had never before experienced what someone else was truly feeling in the middle of a meeting in such an immediate and visceral way.

It is easy to download Slack to your phone, giving you constant contact to short chirpy messages from work. They are the types of messages that you will probably want to read, so managing your notifications is important to set work-life boundaries.

Summary

Communication is a critical soft skill needed as a Salesforce consultant. Knowing how to select the proper medium for any given message will help you become a better communicator. Practice listening and choosing the right words and emojis when speaking and writing. Remember the medium is the message.

Resource

Public Speaking Module on Trailhead, `https://trailhead.salesforce.com/en/content/learn/modules/get_ready_for_dreamforce_become_salesforce_speaker`

Emotional Intelligence

Emotional intelligence is a paramount component of personal and professional success. We all have emotions. We are emotional beings. We cannot avoid having emotions. It is part of who we are. So, it is important to understand the difference between a thought and feeling. It is also critical to recognize the type of feelings that you are having as well as to try to practice empathy for others so that you can try to surmise their perspective and emotions in order to better relate and communicate with them.

Self-awareness is another key component of emotional intelligence. It helps you understand how others perceive you so you can make adjustments in your behavior if needed.

On a Salesforce project, emotional obstacles are common. From navigating through the different stages of team cohesion to making mistakes to managing burnout or even getting removed from a project, these situations are all primed ground for emotional navigation. But fortunately cultivating resilience, optimism, and gratitude help us find balance again.

© Heather Negley 2022
H. Negley, *The Salesforce Consultant's Guide*,
https://doi.org/10.1007/978-1-4842-7960-1_12

What Is Emotional Intelligence?

Emotions and relationships go hand in hand. Awareness of your own emotions and being able to communicate what they are in any given situation is critical to developing emotional intelligence. Consulting is not only intellectually challenging but also can be very emotional. Knowing how to recognize and regulate your emotions is important. Emotional regulation is an attempt to influence the types of emotions that you feel by looking at when you experience emotions and how these emotions are expressed and experienced.[1]

What Is an Emotion?

First things first. A thought is not an emotion. This may seem obvious, or it may not depending on how you perceive the world. Take a moment and ask yourself if you understand the difference. Emotions create bodily sensations and expressive movements. They are not the same thing as thought, although thoughts can certainly trigger emotions. Where do we feel emotions? Well, it depends on the emotion. For example, love and happiness are felt all over, while anger is concentrated in the top half of the body.[2]

The word *emotion* comes from the Latin words for "move out." Literally speaking, it is energy that is moving. Emotions move around our bodies. Believe it or not, if you stop and allow yourself to feel an emotion and do not try to change it, it does not last that long. It moves through you and then out. You do not have to bypass emotions even if they are uncomfortable.

Emotions also give us important information that we need to navigate the world. Base emotions such as anger and fear are physical reactions to things that may hurt us. For example, without anger, you can't establish good boundaries between you and other people or situations. Here is another one: surprise. Surprise helps us remember details. Emotions overlap too. It is possible to feel different degrees of emotions all at once.

Psychologist Robert Plutchik chose eight basic emotions and then divided them up on a wheel (Figure 12-1). Similar to a color wheel, each primary emotion has an opposite and a combination emotion that is a mix of two primaries. There is also an intensity scale that increases as you get toward the center.

---

[1] Gross, JJ, 1988, "Antecedent and response-focused emotion regulation: Divergent consequences for experience, expression and physiology," *Journal of Personality and Social Psychology* 77, pp. 224–237.
[2] Nummenmaa, Lauri, Proceedings of the National Academy of Sciences, Bodily Maps of Emotions, https://www.pnas.org/content/pnas/early/2013/12/26/1321664111.full.pdf

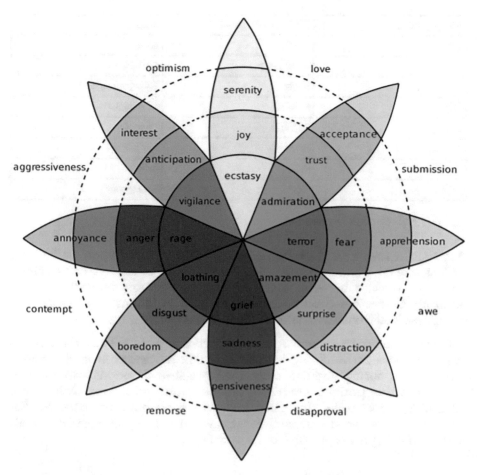

Figure 12-1. Plutchik wheel of emotions (Source: https://www.6seconds.org/2022/03/13/plutchik-wheel-emotions/)

Plutchik's primary emotions paired with their polar opposites are:

- Joy and sadness
- Trust and disgust
- Fear and anger
- Surprise and anticipation

Adding primary emotions together makes a new emotion. These can be seen between the petals on the flower in Figure 12-1, as well as in Figure 12-2.

Base Emotion	Plus Base Emotion	Equals
Joy	Trust	Love
Joy	Anticipation	Optimism
Anticipation	Anger	Aggressiveness
Anger	Disgust	Contempt
Disgust	Sadness	Remorse
Sadness	Surprise	Disapproval
Surprise	Fear	Awe
Fear	Trust	Submission

Figure 12-2. Emotion combinations

As you look down one of the petals, you will see that an emotion can be more or less intense. Plutchik named these varying degrees as well. For example, trust can vacillate between acceptance and admiration depending on the intensity. Cultivate a good vocabulary for your emotions to enhance your emotional intelligence and help build self-awareness.

Different emotions also control different parts of the brain. The left prefrontal region is more active during happiness, while the right prefrontal region is more active during negative emotions.[3] Negative emotions narrow your thinking, while positive emotions broaden your attention. One is not necessarily good while the other bad. We need both perspectives. For instance, a broadened perspective helps you harness your creativity, while narrow thinking helps prepare for fight or flight.

Types of Emotional Turbulence on a Project

Conflicts are going to occur in project work due to group dynamics. There is just no way around it. Implementing software is not straightforward, especially when you are bringing together people who speak business language with people who are speaking a technical language. Emotional events are natural because whenever humans come together, our emotions intertwine. The remainder of the chapter has three emotionally turbulent scenarios that I have seen repeatedly on projects. Like the project archetypes, I have named these *patterns* and offered a perspective to help regulate your emotions through these experiences with self-awareness.

---

[3] Emmons, Robert, *A Thanks: How Practicing Gratitude Can Make you Happier*, p. 74–75

Stormy Seas

As discussed in Chapter 8 in the section "Team Cohesion," in the beginning of a project such as discovery or shortly after, is where the storming stage can cause low team morale. But stormy seas can occur anytime during a project. Be aware of times when new groups are forming and are trying to learn how to work together. Watch out for rigid thinking and confusion that may spur on disappointments and anxiety that runs amok.

Perspective to Take

During stormy seas, it is important to use the emotional consulting tools that you have to manage expectations with your team and the client. A good tool to use when having difficult conversations is appreciation. Strive to show authentic appreciation for the other person's role and contribution to the team. Practice listening, and set a goal to try to do things that will sustain the relationship.

Empathy also goes a long way to making it easier to have difficult conversations. There is nothing more visceral than making a connection with another person through empathy and seeing things from their point of view to try to understand why they are having a particular feeling. Start by asking the person how they are feeling. Attempting to see their point of view to help you understand how they may be viewing you from their perspective. This along with your own self-awareness will help you see the delta, or difference. Perhaps they are perceiving your actions in a different way than you intended. Or vice versa.

Practice being aware of yourself and of the situation. Self-awareness and situational awareness are important components to emotional intelligence. Self-awareness is understanding the thoughts and emotions that are going on inside your body from moment to moment as the situation changes and being able to tell the difference between a thought and an emotion so that you can react accordingly. Self-awareness also gives you a knowingness of what you are good at and the kind of messages that you are communicating through your emotions. Being self-aware helps you be authentic. Acting defensive is a quality of inauthenticity. Learn to notice this in yourself and others. Situational awareness means understanding the norms of an organization and being aware that they are different from place to place. So, what might be acceptable behavior in one organization may be frowned upon in another.

Also, remember to be optimistic. Optimism helps build resilience. Staying positive and striving to reach your potential as well as encouraging others on your team to reach theirs can also bring about happiness. The Greeks called this eudaimonic living. Eudaimonic activities are associated with living in accordance with one's character and producing a positive self-image.[4] There are long-term activities that provide opportunities for personal growth as opposed to short-term or hedonic activities. Passing a Salesforce certification is a eudaimonic activity that should be savored. Savoring is a positive, optimistic activity. Savor the moment to prolong the good experience. Savor your victories. It helps prolong the experience into the future.

Dumpster Fire

A dumpster fire on a Salesforce project happens when everything that can go wrong does go wrong and it stresses you out. There are many types of dumpster fires such as a bad deployment or never-ending user acceptance testing, but one of the most common types is a poor demo. Giving a good demo is a skill that requires practice. It requires an essential combination of public-speaking skills, technical knowledge, communication skills, and confidence.

Live demonstrations of Salesforce functionality can be nerve-wracking, especially when technical issues occur such as when unexpected errors pop up on the screen or an application doesn't work the way you expected it to. But even if you rehearse ahead of time, which you should, and everything works as expected, this doesn't mean that the client will react like you expect. Here are some possible reactions that may catch you off-guard.

The client may say that a piece of functionality is not at all what they were expecting. If this happens, then ask them what they were expecting. Refer back to the acceptance criteria. If their expectation is not in the acceptance criteria, then point out this gap and say that it has to be explicitly stated, but since it's not, we can create a new story and talk through the requirement to close the gap. If it needs more discussion, add it to the action items for follow-up later.

If the person asking for changes is not part of the project team and has not been involved in the project, then tell them you will look into their request. Sometimes demos have a larger audience than just the core stakeholders. Add the request to the action items. After the meeting, escalate this as an issue to your project manager or product owner so they can find out what this person's role is on the project and determine the next best course of action.

Sometimes a client may throw out a random what-if scenario that you honestly do not know the answer to. Good consultants are honest and tell clients if they don't know an answer. It's okay to say that this question falls outside the

[4] https://www.psychologytoday.com/us/blog/what-doesnt-kill-us/201901/what-is-eudaimonic-happiness

scope of your planned presentation today and you are not prepared to talk in depth on it, but you can have a discussion later about it. If you understand what the question is but don't know the answer, you can simply say that you don't know, but you will research it or consult with a colleague to find an answer and/or options and get back to them. If you don't understand the question, don't spend a lot of time trying to analyze it in the middle of a demo. Instead suggest having further discussions with them to make sure you understand the scenario. We all need time to think and process information, so if you do, it is okay to communicate this. It's important to follow up later if this is your answer. Make sure you announce it as an action item at the end of the presentation.

At the end of the meeting, if the application did not work correctly or you feel like you stumbled through things, don't over-apologize for all the mistakes that you think you have made. It may not be as bad as you initially feel it is. It's okay to apologize; just don't overdo it. Do read back the list of action items and make a commitment to get them answered and/or set up a time for further discussion. And do this in a timely manner. Tell them you are committed to finding the best solution to help them have a successful project and make sure you are authentic and mean it.

If the client wants things solutioned a certain way but you know their request is not an ideal solution, remember you are not an order taker. You are a trusted adviser, and to act like a trusted adviser you need to have the self-confidence and emotional intelligence to tell a client something they may not want to hear in a way that they know you have their best interest in mind. This goes back to selecting the right word such as "unconventional" rather than "wrong" or "Yes, but…," listening with empathy and knowing the project archetype that you are in and responding accordingly.

If the client insists on something that is out of scope, there are several ways to handle this. If you know it is out of scope, you can say that you could do it as part of another project but not this one. If they don't accept this answer or if you are not sure if it is out of scope, you can ask them for a follow-up meeting later and then proceed with your demo. Add this to the action items, and announce it at the end of the presentation.

Perspective to Take

If you do make a mistake on a demo or somewhere else on a project, don't beat yourself up for doing a bad job. Mistakes are a normal part of the learning process. You really can't expect perfection from yourself no matter how much experience you have. That's idealistic thinking and not realistic. For example, I have seen brilliant consultants give demos with broken calculations because the developers were working during the demo and had turned off a flow in order to make changes, thereby inactivating the calculations.

See mistakes for what they are: a chance to learn more, a chance to fine-tune what you know, a chance to see the gap in your knowledge and build that bridge that makes it complete, a chance to become an even better consultant than you already are. In the previous example, the consultant instituted a code freeze during all demos and told developers to do something else during that time. Making mistakes is part of the path to excellence. Great athletes and other successful leaders have great stories about their failures. Here is a quote on failing from basketball legend Michael Jordon:

> "I've missed more than 9,000 shots in my career. I've lost almost 300 games. Twenty-six times I've been trusted to take the game-winning shot and missed. I've failed over and over and over again in my life. And that is why I succeed."

It is hard to see with that kind of perspective in the moments of emotional turmoil, but be patient with yourself and keep trying. Remember anytime you try something new and fail, you learn and grow faster than if you succeed without failing. Failing can be painful, but learning the value of failing is worth it. Mistakes are part of the learning process of becoming a consultant. They are lessons that stick around.

You may not have control of how the client reacts in a dumpster fire, but you do have control over how you react to your thoughts. Rational emotive behavior therapy, developed by Albert Ellis, is a form of cognitive behavior therapy in which the central approach is based on ancient Stoic philosophers who discovered that people are not affected by external events but by their thinking of events.[5] He taught the advantages of identifying irrational beliefs and negative thought patterns to achieve self-acceptance. See the "Resources" section for a link to his website and to learn more about how to examine and challenge unhealthy thinking.

So if you leave a meeting with negative feelings, especially if you really did make a mistake or were caught off-guard and said the wrong thing, pay attention to your thinking. Perhaps you will experience catastrophic thinking and ruminating thoughts about worst-case scenarios. This type of thinking can lead to anxiety. Anxiety triggers the fight or flight response and is a physiological reaction that in part makes your heart rate and breathing rate increase. Many times the fight-or-flight response can seem like an overreaction to a situation. Anxiety is actually a bodily response to danger. The amygdala, part of the brain responsible for triggering the fight or flight response, is part of the limbic system, which is linked to the processing of emotions. It constantly scans the environment. When it is triggered, the fight or flight response

---

[5] Ellis, Albert (1997). *The practice of rational emotive behavior therapy* (2nd ed.). New York, N.Y.: Springer Publishing Company. p. 112. ISBN 0826154719. OCLC 35223015.

activates, getting your muscles ready to fight or run away from a potential threat. It is a really great response system for running away from a sabertooth tiger. In modern times sometimes it's too good and gets triggered when you really don't need it to, like when you are trying to give a presentation to an audience. If only we could update the amygdala code with conditional logic, something like "If giving a presentation, then do nothing."

Anxiety is also a coping mechanism to resisting emotions. In other words, anxiety covers up the underlying emotions that our bodies do not want us to feel. The ones it has decided are much worse to feel like sadness. It blocks emotions.[6]

Anxiety is set off by catastrophic thinking that overestimates the probability of something bad happening. This worry triggers the amygdala, and you are ready to run even if there is no threat around. These triggering thoughts can occur over and over again and keep retriggering the amygdala. If it is not triggered again, the anxiety will dissipate. You have to catch the triggering thoughts, though, and sometimes that is easier said than done. If the thoughts keep going around in circles, it is called *rumination* and can keep retriggering the fight-or-flight response.

But with a little practice, you can control how you react to your thoughts. Start by reaching out to your mentor, manager, or a friend to talk about your thoughts and feelings. When asking for help, try to not feel guilty about wanting to talk. Asking for help doesn't mean you are needy, and it's okay to give up a little control to receive help. It may introduce a new dynamic in your thought pattern and be just what you need to help stop retriggering your amygdala and stop the ruminating thoughts.[7] Connection with others is something that humans are wired to do. We are innately social. We need each other, like bees who make hives. We make cities with skyscrapers so we can all live next to each other and help each other run the city. Yes, even if you are an introvert, you still need human connection, because human connection is essential for human well-being.

Daily meditation is also a good practice to manage anxiety. It brings your attention to the present and helps release emotions that have gotten stored in your body throughout the days and weeks. Breathing techniques can interrupt stress hormones. Learning to invite your emotions in and breathing slowly as you experience them helps transmute or change them so they dissipate. Move around to help emotions move around your body better and

[6] Cushnir, Raphael, The Truth About Anxiety, https://www.psychologytoday.com/us/blog/emotional-connection/201107/the-truth-about-anxiety-0
[7] Stieg, Cor, Everyone needs help during the coronavirus pandemic- here's the psychological reason why asking for help is so hard, CNBC https://www.cnbc.com/2020/04/22/why-asking-for-help-is-so-hard-and-how-to-get-better-at-it.html

not get stuck. Remember, they are there for your protection and are trying to tell you something. You should feel an emotion, but this doesn't mean you need to act out a response to the behavior.

Burnt

You want to avoid becoming torched to a crisp and burned out on a project. Managing burnout is all about creating balance in your life. Projects have slow times and fast times. I call these peaks and valleys. Different roles are busy at different times. Generally speaking, project managers have the most work in the beginning in the planning stages while developers are busier toward the end during deployments. But burnout can occur at any time, especially if you are traveling a lot, working more than 40 hours a week on a continuous basis, or the project has an extended storming stage, which may cause continued and unmanageable emotional turbulence.

My friend, Kai, has experienced his share of burnout. He has worked with Salesforce for more than a decade, first as a sales leader and later as an executive for a successful Salesforce systems integrator. Working more than 40 hours a week was always the norm for Kai. What started as a normal gig evolved into managing multiple departments and dozens of employees, all the while helping to steer the growth strategy for one of the fastest-growing companies in the ecosystem.

At first, when he was in his 30s, Kai didn't mind working more than 40 hours a week and thought it seemed normal like a "badge of honor." After work, everyone would start texting, and it felt like the fervor in which he worked just spread to his co-workers. Plus, it was fun. There were a lot of after-work activities that came from being courted by ISV partners or other happy hours, parties, and ball games for clients. The days and nights just bled together. During 2010–2013, he estimates that a typical week was easily more like 50–60 hours. And with his daughter's birth in 2011, the demands on his time just increased, and he kept going at this pace.

Then in 2013, he added travel and another child to this mix. You can probably see where this is going. His company opened a Chicago office, so the trips increased, and his son was born. Between 2013 and 2018, his pace was so frenetic that he says it just felt like a "blur." He was traveling every week mostly between Labor Day and Memorial Day, which is nine months out of the year. The trips were often to multiple destinations as well to see as many people as possible in the shortest amount of time. In order to maximize time with his family, he would take red-eye or 6 a.m. flights. If he wasn't already suffering from sleep deprivation before, he definitely was now.

Burnout is gradual and sometimes hard to identify right away, especially if there are underlying medical issues. Kai thinks he was in denial about it when he took medical leave in 2018. He made an attempt to try to balance his work-life time. He took two months off that year and felt great afterward. Almost immediately, he dove back into work as if nothing had changed. Dreamforce was a few weeks after he came back, and Kai ended up with an upper respiratory infection for almost six months afterward. Then the pandemic hit, and while the travel stopped, the changes and challenges wore on his physical and mental health. He finally realized, after thoughtful consideration with his company's leadership, that he had to change every aspect of his work life, starting with another medical leave of absence. Upon his return, he scaled way back on his work responsibilities and started a daily meditation routine. He also completely overhauled his diet and set a daily exercise goal. His daily step goal is 10,000 minimum. He also makes sure he gets enough sleep, talks to a clinical psychologist on a weekly basis, and has adopted a holistic perspective on his medical care rather than managing symptoms.

See the "Resources" section for Kai's recommendations and his explanation in his words on why they were helpful to him on his journey.

Perspective to Take

Annoyance, anger, and stress are common when you are burned out. And emotions can intensify if left unacknowledged. An annoyance can turn into anger. It is important to assign your emotions a label so you can monitor their intensity to see if they are getting more or less intense. Then take intentional steps to create more nonwork time around you to address the issue that you have identified to help manage the burnout. Whether it is traveling less, taking a vacation, going for a run, or using another stress management tool, aim for balance.

Booted

One of the most challenging experiences that can happen to a consultant is being removed from a project. It hurts and can be tough to maneuver through. But this event, like mistakes, are great learning experiences and make you stronger. Consultants get removed from projects for many reasons. Sometimes the firm cannot sell anything and therefore cannot afford to pay you anymore. Other times you may be assigned to a project that stretches your skills, and you make mistakes or can't effectively communicate with the client. You may not receive enough management support, and you are blamed rather than coached. Sometimes the client wants a different consultant for reasons outside your control. Or it's just too tough a crowd for you to know how to manage. If your emotional intelligence is not fully developed, your self-awareness may not be astute enough to accurately "read the room," and you may come across differently and in a way that you don't realize. It may spiral out of your control. Or you may not know how to do the role, but you don't want to stop trying because you don't like to quit things, but you have run out of time for some reason.

Whatever the reason, there is a cognitive dissonance between the courting that is done by recruiters and managers who want to hire you at the beginning of the employment process and the forced "goodbyes" at the end. There are a whole variety of behaviors from managers at the end and a whole range of ways you may react to the change. Since these are not everyday events, you probably don't have a lot of practice, and this can be a tough thing to manage emotionally.

First, the good news—just because you are removed from a project doesn't necessarily mean that you are out of a job. If you work for a reputable consulting firm and generally do a good job on projects, then the firm will most likely find you another project. But if the circumstances are such that the firm doesn't think you can add value then, then they may ask you to leave the firm entirely.

Unfortunately, there are people in this world who do not know how to empathize. It is not your job to teach them how to. It is, however, important for you to protect yourself from people who are not communicating with empathy when you are. Sometimes someone who lacks empathy can subtly bully or gaslight a person. Gaslighting can feel like very calculated manipulation. It is insidious and gets ahead of you before you realize what is happening. It can occur in the workplace because power structures are common. There are things you can do to protect yourself. A deep delve into gaslighting is outside the scope of this book, but I have left a few resources at the end of this chapter if you feel that you have encountered this behavior at work.

Perspective to Take

Oftentimes business decisions and empathy or human-centric decisions are opposite sides of a coin, but on the bright side, after a bad event, positive emotions will be there to help you move on. Learn to cultivate positive emotions by taking purposeful actions.

We all have resilience, and there are things we can do to enhance it. It may seem counterintuitive to seek out positive emotions after you have been kicked off a project. You should definitely take time to acknowledge and process the negative ones that are there to tell you that you have been hurt. But remember positive and negative emotions influence thoughts. Experiencing positive emotions increases resilience. Finding positive emotion such as humor in the middle of a stressful situation can really help move you away from the negative feelings. A support network of family and friends is also important to have. Use resilience to move on.

Love and gratitude are key components in resilience, and this is what you want to feel from your support network. Practicing regular grateful thinking leads to increased happiness. Thanking a person in your support network is an act of gratitude and a step toward a positive feeling.

Gratitude requires action to thank another person for their part for the positive outcomes in your life. It helps you go outside yourself, unlike depression, which is an emotion that keeps your thoughts internal. The act of reaching out to someone to give thanks reinforces the idea that we need people and can't do everything ourselves.

According to Robert A Emmons, PHD, and author of *Thanks*,

> "Gratitude takes us outside ourselves where we see ourselves as part of a larger, intricate network of sustaining relationships, relationships that are mutually reciprocal…"

> "…Gratitude drives out toxic emotions of resentment, anger and envy and may be associated with better long term emotional and physical health."

Perhaps it was in utilizing the skill of resilience to feel positive emotions that led humans to start making stone tools. The person who created the first stone tool lived in Tanzania, Africa, nearly two million years ago. The Olduvai stone chopping tool is a stone that has been chipped away to give way to a sharp edge. This person who made this thought there was a better way to do something, and creating this tool allowed the person to have more experiences with meaning and purpose. This chopping tool and the ones made after changed a lot of things for humans living at that time. The tool helped them to strip the meat off animal bones and consume more protein including the bone marrow, which helped their brains grow. It also allowed them to travel far from home because they could use it to strip the branches off trees. Eventually, humans started to depend on it. It was the first technology, and we have been utilizing this flexible adaptation through refining and resilience ever since.

Summary

From an emotionally chaotic project to making mistakes, managing your emotions on a project can be challenging. Remember, a feeling is how you experience an emotion. It is not the same thing as a thought. Practice empathy to traverse difficult relationships. Maintain balance in your lifestyle to avoid burnout. Manage anxiety by remembering your thoughts are triggering your emotions. Be mindful of the content of your thoughts. Most important, if you get the wind knocked out of you unexpectedly on a bad project, remember that you are human, and that means you have resilience. You can cultivate optimism. You can grow. You can learn. You can rise up stronger than before and try again.

Resources

The Albert Ellis Institute, cognitive behavior therapy that examines and explores ways to challenge unhelpful thinking, `https://albertellis.org/rebt-cbt-therapy/`

Ten Tips to Help You Stop Ruminating, `https://www.healthline.com/health/how-to-stop-ruminating`

Qoya, free movement videos to help unstick stuck energy, `https://www.qoya.love/movement-videos`

VIA Survey of Character Strengths, a free and quick assessment to help you understand your best qualities, `https://www.authentichappiness.sas.upenn.edu/questionnaires/survey-character-strengths`

The Resilience Factor: 7 Keys to Finding Your Inner Strength and Overcoming Life's Hurdles, a book by psychologists Karen Reivich and Andrew Shatte who teach the importance of resilience and how to improve this innate skill, `https://www.amazon.com/dp/B000FBJCQC/ref=dp-kindle-redirect?_encoding=UTF8&btkr=1`

7 Signs of Gaslighting at the Workplace, `https://www.psychologytoday.com/us/blog/communication-success/202007/7-signs-gaslighting-the-workplace`

That's Not What Happened! How to Deal with Gaslighting in the Workplace, `https://www.jucm.com/thats-not-what-happened-how-to-deal-with-gaslighting-in-the-workplace/`

Meditation Resources

Tara Brach, PhD, is an internationally known meditation teacher. On her Tara Brach podcast, Tara shares stories and meditations that blend Western psychology and Eastern spiritual practices. She teaches the value of mindfulness, meditation, and self-compassion in relieving emotional suffering, serving spiritual awakening, and bringing healing to the world, `https://podcasts. apple.com/us/podcast/tara-brach/id265264862`

Meditation Trailhead Module from Salesforce, `https://trailhead. salesforce.com/content/learn/modules/mindful-living`

Headspace.com, app started by Andy Puddicombe who cut short his sports science degree to become a Buddhist monk; it has guided meditations, animations, articles, and videos

Calm.com, an app for sleep, mediation, and self-improvements with video lessons in mindful movement and gentle stretching, sleep stories, nature scenes, and sounds for working, studying, or sleeping as well as audio programs

Kai's Recommendations for Managing Burnout

These are resources that Kai used to manage his burnout, including his perspective on what he specifically found useful in them.

`https://www.parsleyhealth.com/`: "Through Parsley, I learned that I can take control of my health and focus on wellness and prevention. Previously, relying solely on western medicine to relieve symptoms never cured my underlying conditions."

Letting Go, The Pathway of Surrender by Dr David Hawkins : "To change your life in any capacity, you have to be willing to let the things that consume you go. A very tall task for any person, but having the awareness is key to being able to make the change necessary. Someone I met on my meditation journey introduced me to this book, and it changed my life."

Transcendental Meditation: "This is my personal preference for meditation but the key is to find something that works for you consistently."

Critical Thinking and Problem-Solving Skills

Critical thinking is a type of systematic thinking that is used to solve problems using logic. The first step is to gather the information needed to help you solve your problem. You start by analyzing and evaluating sources for authority to give you the best shot at finding something truthful and unbiased. Watch Out For information overload. Access to information is easier than ever these days, and it is easy to get overwhelmed by it all. As you conduct your research, keep your information organized by filtering, synthesizing, and distilling it. And keep your effort timeboxed. Start broad enough to obtain a wide berth, like a fisherman casting a large net into an ocean. This helps find multiple points of view. But don't spend more time than necessary. Practicing collecting what is sufficient to answer your questions.

© Heather Negley 2022
H. Negley, *The Salesforce Consultant's Guide*,
https://doi.org/10.1007/978-1-4842-7960-1_13

Learn to skim information for key points and use the search feature in documents to find relevant keywords. Finally, watch out for cognitive biases that are thinking traps that humans have a tendency to fall into under specific circumstances. There are more than 180 cognitive biases, and the list grows all the time. You don't have to memorize every one, but you should have a good reference resource to monitor from time to time and see if any of them apply in your present situation. You'll find good source for cognitive biases in this chapter.

What Is Critical Thinking?

Critical thinking helps people solve problems systematically using facts and data. It involves going through a process of gathering information, analyzing, evaluating, and synthesizing the information to help solve problems in a timely manner. Logic plays a predominant role in critical thinking, because the goal of critical thinking is to solve problems well and not in a haphazard manner.

Gathering, Analyzing, Evaluating

Gathering and analyzing information is the first step in problem solving. The main goal in gathering information is to collect enough truthful and accurate information for later analysis. This analysis will be utilized to solve the problem. When you are collecting information, you need to check the authority of your source. An authoritative source is one where the author has the knowledge and experience that qualifies them to communicate as an expert on a given subject. In the academic community, authority is indicated by credentials, previously published works on the subject, institutional affiliation, awards, imprint, reviews, patterns of citation, etc.[1]

On a Salesforce project, you want to make sure you are talking to the most knowledgeable person on the subject in the context of the problem that you are trying to solve. For example, during discovery you are usually analyzing current business processes and technologies. There may be many business processes with many specialists. Make sure you are talking to the most knowledgeable expert. If you are not sure, then ask them if there is anyone else they think you should talk to on topics that you should know about for project success. On the technology side, there is usually a group of people who understand how the system architecture of the organization is constructed. You want to divide your questions up by their specialties and record the information in a systematic fashion. If you are researching best practices in the industry, look for the most knowledgeable people and trusted sources in a specific specialty of Salesforce to help you gather pertinent information to analyze.

---

[1] Reitz, Joan. Online Dictionary for Library and Information Science: Accessed 11/07/2021

Watch Out For

Bias

As you start to analyze the information that you have collected, you need to evaluate it for bias and inaccuracies. Examine the assumptions that the sources make and determine if they align with the assumptions for the problem at hand. Use logic to determine if you have a gap in your assumptions or if the assumptions are biased, irrelevant, or inaccurate.

Differentiate an Opinion from a Fact

Stay away from biased opinions when doing research unless you want to show two sides of an issue and the argument for each side. Just make sure you present the research as opinions and not facts. Provide balanced information back to the client.

The Internet is a useful tool for gathering information. But sources like Wikipedia are not considered authoritative. Wikipedia may reference authoritative sources, but each one should be evaluated independently for authority. Salesforce itself has a plethora of good resources and should be considered authoritative for Salesforce consulting research. There are various experts in the field, some of which are mentioned in this guidebook. In general, try to get the answer to your research questions from multiple sources to see if patterns emerge. If you are looking for industry research, then look to industry reports such as Gartner, which publishes a series of market research reports for the IT industry called the Magic Quadrant.

Conducting interviews from experts is another good way to gather truthful information. You may do this during discovery with subject matter experts on the client side. Or you may interview other Salesforce consultants to get recommendations of authoritative resources.

Information Overload

There is a balance between not having enough information and having too much. Consuming too much information is called *information overload*. Futurist Alvin Toffler popularized the term in his famous book from 1970, *Future Shock*. He said,

> People of the future may suffer not from an absence of choice but from a paralysing surfeit of it. They may turn out to be victims of that peculiarly super-industrial dilemma: overchoice.

In Salesforce project work, discovery is the most common time for information overload to happen. Information overload occurs when you are inundated by an avalanche of information in what feels like an unorganized flood that is impossible to process and feels overwhelming. A popular business idiom, "drinking from the firehouse," alludes to this predicament. Being exposed to too much information can impede your systemic process to problem solving, and it is important to learn to become aware of when it is happening so you can manage it.

In Salesforce project work, it's easy to become consumed and distracted by the small things when you are gathering an excessive amount of information. Toffler also said,

> ...You've got to think about big things while you're doing small things, so that all the small things go in the right direction...

Remember the goals of the project. Salesforce project work is very detailed. Don't lose sight of what you are trying to accomplish and by when.

Strategies to Help

There are several things you can do to manage information overload. Here are some tips to manage information overload on a Salesforce project.

Gather Relevant Information. For example, during a discovery meeting, take notes, but don't try to write a transcript of everything the person is saying.

You don't have to consume every piece of information. Learn to skim. Separate the signal from the noise. Consume information in an orderly way. Allow it to queue and process it on a regular basis. It doesn't need to be in real time unless there is a specific reason to do so.

Don't record every meeting. Doing so will create an enormous amount of noise and can take a long time to go back and listen to. Do record key meetings where detailed information is shared and has high value where the information is not going to change frequently such as current state business processes. You don't need to record status meetings where updates change every day. Strive for balance. Prioritize value over quantity.

Make Information Clear to Understand. Capture the key points and make a separate section in your notes for action items and next steps.

Filter information through the use of categorizing. Tag notes with categories to help you with the synthesis process. See the next section for more on this.

Delegate information-gathering responsibilities to other people on your team. Don't go it alone. Ask everyone to chip in and compare notes. You may even want to use the same notes document by sharing a document using Google Docs or another tool. Type notes together in real time in a discovery meeting so multiple versions of a document are not created and so you don't have to go back and combine all the separate documents into a single source later. Instead, use one document and create sections for each person to enter their notes. Try not to solution during discovery. Focus on gathering the information before you design.

Time Management

Timebox information-gathering discussions. Create an outline or agenda of the topics that you would like to cover during a session. During the meeting, redirect the group when participants go down unnecessary "rabbit holes" or "detailed tangents" and suggest setting aside these topics in a parking lot. A parking lot is just a list of items that need further discussion at a later time. After the meeting, decide how much time you should allocate to follow-up discussions around the items and if they are needed or not. Determine which items are required inputs for the analysis stage and prioritize those first.

Synthesizing and Distilling

Another key component of critical thinking involves synthesizing and distilling information into manageable, logical chunks to help with problem solving. The chunks of information are then compared and contrasted using various metrics, calculations, and equations. For example, after you compare one chunk of information with another, it can be analyzed as a Boolean and visualized using a Venn diagram. Figure 13-1 illustrates how a Venn diagram can communicate distilled analysis. In this example, the project team analyzed the client's business processes in the customer success, marketing, and sales departments and came to the conclusion that the marketing department had business processes that overlapped with customer success and sales.

The project team found that there was duplicate effort occurring in silos and recommended a more streamlined approach where the three departments would share information in an omnichannel or multichannel to offer a unified 360-degree view of information for all three teams and customers.

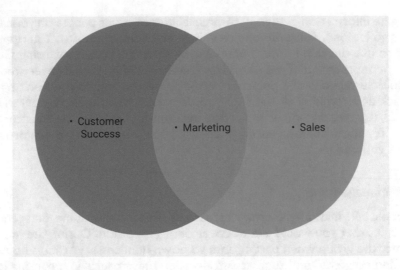

Figure 13-1. *Venn diagram*

Matrixes are another useful tool to utilize to organize information in a structured way. Synthesize the information by bringing it together from all the sources into one matrix, which will help you keep it organized. Distill it by eliminating extraneous or duplicate information. The tags that you created in your notes can be used as column headers in your spreadsheet and then grouped and filtered to compare and contrast and identify patterns.

For example, the matrix in Figure 13-2 helps you see the logical connections between ideas to deduce consequences. In this example, the consultant learned that the marketing team would like to create new contacts that they receive from meeting people at conferences. But during an interview with the sales team, the sales manager indicated that the only roles that needed to add new contacts were the sales and customer success teams. By creating a matrix, to analyze this information, you can see that the two requirements are in direct conflict with one another. According to the following analysis, the marketing department can only read the records on the contact object. They cannot create new records. This discrepancy should be discussed with the product owner so that the business can make a collaborative decision.

Profile	Accounts	Contacts	Opportunities
Admin	CRED	CRED	CRED
Marketing	R	R	R
Sales	CRE	CRE	CRE
Customer Success	CRE	CRE	CRE
C=Create, R=Read, E=Edit, D=Delete			

Figure 13-2. *Matrix*

Try to understand the reasons behind decisions. In this example, the consultant may want to ask why they want the marketing department to have read-only access. Their answer may be that they don't see a need for it, but if the marketing department explains that they need to create access to help sales have contact information to more people and potential opportunities, then the sales team may agree. Sometimes Salesforce consultants may recommend starting with an open org where all users are given access to create, read, and edit all objects, and then they ask stakeholders why a persona should not have access to a piece of information. If the stakeholders cannot think of a reason, everyone has access. If a reason comes up later, it can be discussed, and access and/or viewability can be restricted later.

Cognitive Biases

Sometimes our thinking fails us, and we inadvertently fall into a blind spot or a cognitive bias. There are more than 180 cognitive biases. The Cognitive Bias Codex, designed by John Manoogian III and Buster Benson breaks down the cognitive errors into four main categories of information overload, meaning, memory and speed. The link in the resources section will take you to a large version of the Codex. The Codex is very detailed. I encourage you to visit the link. I have highlighted some biases that you may encounter on a Salesforce project in this chapter, but it is in no way an exhaustive list. I recommend reading through the codex and referring to it from time to time. It is updated often.

Bike-Shedding Effect(Parkinson's Law of Triviality)

The bike-shedding effect is the argument that people in an organization may give disproportionate weight to trivial issues. It was first identified by C. Northcote Parkinson in 1957 who gave the example of a group of people at a nuclear power plant who spent the majority of their time discussing minor but easy-to-understand issues such as what color the bicycle shed should be while ignoring the overall design plan for the plant itself. You may encounter this behavior on a Salesforce project if, for example, a client is overly focused on the user interface help text rather than making sure they have enough data to complete the critical path of the application. Or if they are overly focused on a minor edge case that affects 1 percent of the users instead of focusing on the main design of their application, which affects all of their users and is needed to achieve project goals. Minor, noncritical edge cases should be solved outside the main design of the system. Sure, there might be some high-risk edge cases that force a major design decision, but most of the time minor, noncritical edge cases are for a small number of users and are exceptions outside the happy path. Software development is iterative. Build for the happy path for the majority of the users. This means to spend time evaluating the use cases that apply to the majority of the users, the core requirements.

Information Bias

Information bias is when someone thinks that gathering more information will make it easier to make the decision when in fact additional information is not needed to make a decision. For example, on a Salesforce project, this bias may come up when the team is trying to make design decisions. There is a law of diminishing return that happens with examining every use case and solution done in the past that is similar to the one you are researching. Time has a way of making information stale, and old solutions don't necessarily work in the present moment. Salesforce is constantly publishing new releases, and the best way to do things is constantly changing and evolving.

Irrational Escalation (Escalation of Commitment)

This is a pattern where people when faced with a negative outcome over and over again from a previous decision continue to act in the same manner rather than alter their course. An example of this behavior on a Salesforce project could be if a client has a strategy for retrieving the source of the data they want to use in their application, but for one reason or another fails to produce it. Maybe they cannot gain access to it after all, but instead of changing their strategy, they maintain actions that are irrational but align with their previous decision.

Automation Bias

Automation bias occurs when people over-rely on automated functionality and stop thinking through what the automation is doing. In Chapter 4, I explained the benefits of humans working with automated systems. This is one of the reasons. Programs are not perfect. Automation does not solve every problem. There is still a need for error handling and monitoring and placing value on the things that humans can do to supplement the automation. For example, integration errors can occur on a batch upload that is processed nightly. Just because it worked perfectly the night before doesn't mean it will work perfectly the next night. The program will produce error reports that must be reviewed by a human to figure out why the error happened and correct the mistake. It could be something as simple as a calculation field being wrong after a certain amount of time because of the formula that was used. Maybe the formula counted up to 100 days and on the 101st day it didn't know what to do, so it didn't update a record, and an error was reported. A human needs to analyze the error and decide if the code needs to be refactored to avoid this from happening again.

Next in Line Effect

This is when the moment it is your turn to talk or present your mind goes blank. This may happen the instance the meeting is turned over to you. You need to present a demo and despite practicing the day before and having notes in front of you, you can't recall any information. This is a bummer if this has happened to you, but now you know—it's just a common human flaw and not your own personal defect.

Spacing Effect

The spacing effect is the consequence where you learn more if you spread out your learning over a period of time rather than trying to cram it all into a short session. This is a good tip to keep in mind when you are studying for a certification. Give yourself the proper amount of time.

Semmelweis Reflex

This is when new evidence is rejected because it contradicts established norms. You may encounter this type of thinking on a stick in the mud project, described in Chapter 10, where stakeholders are resistant to change.

Summary

Critical thinking is an important skill to master and takes lots of practice. As you gather information to analyze, keep it organized and don't spend too much time looking for information you may not need to solve the problem. Know when enough is enough. Manage information overload. Use a balanced approach if you want to show opinions. Separate a fact that comes from an authoritative source from an opinion when presenting analysis.

Finally, watch out for cognitive biases. Use the Cognitive Bias Codex with definitions image to monitor cognitive biases, and ask yourself if you have recently encountered any.

Resources

The Pyramid Principle: Logic in Writing and Thinking by Barbara Minto, `https://www.amazon.com/Pyramid-Principle-Logic-Writing-Thinking/dp/0273710516`

Cognitive Bias Codex with Definitions, an enormous image that takes up your whole browser window and lists the definitions of each cognitive bias. Use the magnifying glass in your browser to zoom in and out of the infographic to read the biases and their definitions grouped by quadrants and further subdivided. For example, the subcategories in the Information Overload quadrant are as follows:

- We notice things already primed in memory or repeated often (12 biases).

- Bizarre, funny, visually striking, or anthropomorphic things stick out more than nonbizarre/unfunny things (six biases)

- We notice when something has changed (eight biases)

- We are drawn to details that confirm our own existing beliefs (13 biases, including the Semmelweis Reflex mentioned earlier)

- We notice flaws in others more easily than we notice flaws in ourselves (three biases).

`https://upload.wikimedia.org/wikipedia/commons/c/ce/Cognitive_Bias_Codex_With_Definitions%2C_an_Extension_of_the_work_of_John_Manoogian_by_Brian_Morrissette.jpg`

APPENDIX

A

Other Resources

Blog by a Salesforce developer who has been in the ecosystem since 2011, https://www.infallibletechie.com/

Resource to practice coding, https://www.sfdc99.com/

Salesforce Women in Tech, Twitter @SFDCWiT, private group for woman in Salesforce, https://trailblazers.salesforce.com/_ui/core/chatter/groups/GroupProfilePage?g=0F9300000001oES

Salesforce Ben, run by Ben McCarthy, a good place to keep up with changes in the Salesforce ecosystem and with lots of useful content that is constantly updated, https://www.salesforceben.com/

Find answers to questions from the community and Salesforce Stack Exchange, https://trailblazers.salesforce.com/answers, https://salesforce.stackexchange.com/

Slack group called Salesforce #ohanaSlack run by Meighan Brodkey, https://meighanrockssf.com/2019/04/02/salesforce-ohana-slack/

Toolkit for common Salesforce consulting processes and tasks, https://cloudtoolkit.co/

Salesforce MVP Salesforce nomination program for people in the ecosystem who give back to the community in a significant way, https://www.salesforce.com/blog/nominate-trailblazer-mentors-salesforce-mvp/?d=7010M000001yv8PQAQ

© Heather Negley 2022
H. Negley, *The Salesforce Consultant's Guide*,
https://doi.org/10.1007/978-1-4842-7960-1

Who Sees What Video Series from Salesforce, covers the main features in Salesforce that determine the visibility of data and access to that data, https://www.youtube.com/watch?v=GOIPHOaLYOE

Paid Practice Exams, https://focusonforce.com/admin-study-guide/

Free Practice Questions, https://quizlet.com/subject/salesforce/

Config Workbook, a paid AppExchange product that helps you extract Salesforce metadata in Excel files, http://www.configworkbook.com/

Index

A

Acceptance criteria, 37, 59, 87, 101

Agile 101, 88

Agile ceremonies, 35, 99, 100, 105

Agile projects, 34, 35, 40, 43, 44, 96

Airline clubs, 74

Analytical Engine, 50

Apex, 40, 50

Apex Hours, 53

Assumptions, 57, 63, 65–67, 106, 107

Automated testing, 52, 94

Automation bias, 158

Automation Hour, 53

Awareness, Desire, Knowledge, Ability, and
Reinforcement (Adkar), 46

B

Backlog, 99–101

Backlog grooming, 100, 101

Backlog refinement
clouds, 102
definition, 100
definition of ready, 100
dependencies, 101, 102
design, 101, 102
epics, 100
product owner, 100, 101

rules, 100
stories, 100, 101

Bernoulli numbers, 50

Bike-shedding effect, 157, 158

Blocker, 105

Breathing techniques, 143

Bugs, 108, 110

Business analysis
acceptance criteria, 94
current/future state, 91, 92
definition, 91
process flows, 92, 93
user stories, 93

Business analysts, 6, 22, 45, 47, 52, 54,
61, 81, 90

Business architect, 45

C

Centralized staffing model, 60, 61

Certified technical architect (CTA), 47, 48

Change manager, 46, 54

CLEAR program, 73

Client management, 116

Cognitive behavior therapy, 142, 158

Cognitive Bias Codex, 157, 160

Communication method, 46, 129
listening, 130, 131
The medium is the message, 129

© Heather Negley 2022
H. Negley, *The Salesforce Consultant's Guide*,
https://doi.org/10.1007/978-1-4842-7960-1

Printed in the United States
by Baker & Taylor Publisher Services